PRAISE FOR SHANNON KAISER

"Shannon Kaiser is an incredible woman on a mission to help people find peace, happiness and fulfillment in their lives. Her desire to serve othe es through all of her work."
—**Gabı in,** New York Times Bestselling Author: *May Cause Mirac.*

"I love this! Shannon's s sunny and bright and will light your day with heart and blis.
—**Kristine Carlson,** New York Times Bestselling Author: *Don't Sweat the Small Stuff for Women and Moms.*

"Shannon is a modern thought leader on the rise."
—**Café Truth**

"Shannon Kaiser not only believes in the message of happiness, she lives it and breathes it. Every time I talk to Shannon, happiness finds a way in.
— **Christine Arylo,** author of *Madly in Love with ME.*

"For many of us, feeling excited and fulfilled on a day-to-day basis can seem impossible. If you are in search for lasting happiness, then let this truly remarkable woman guide you. She reminds us all that life is supposed to be exciting, fun and fulfilling."
— *IDEAL Magazine*

"Shannon Kaiser is a prolific writer who inspires thousands every week."
—**Mind Body Green**

ALSO BY SHANNON KAISER

Books:

Adventures for Your Soul
21 Ways to Transform Your Habits and Reach Your Full Potential
(Berkley Press, Penguin, Available May 2015)

Find Your Happy
An Inspirational Guide to Loving Life to Its Fullest
(Balboa Press, 2012, International Bestseller)

Instant Inspiration
(eBook available on the authors website)

Audio CD Meditation Albums:

I am Fearless
Empowering meditations for inner peace, confidence and clarity.

Find Your Happy Motivational Mantras
Audio meditations to help you live your life to the fullest.

Clear Your Fear
Meditations to help remove barriers keeping you from bliss.

Courses

Embrace Your Single Self, an 8- week Daily Om
online course (www.dailyom.com)

*All of the books above are available at your local bookstore
or favorite online book retailer. The audio CDs are available
on iTunes or Amazon.com. You can order all of these titles
through the authors website www.playwiththeworld.com.*

Find Your Happy Daily Mantras

365 Days of Motivation for a Happy, Peaceful and Fulfilling Life.

SHANNON KAISER

BALBOA.
PRESS

A DIVISION OF HAY HOUSE

Jacket cover design by: Shannon Kaiser
Internal art direction: Shannon Kaiser
Jacket photograph: Nick Ray/ Her Lovely Heart

Balboa Press books may be ordered through booksellers or by contacting:

Balboa Press
A Division of Hay House
1663 Liberty Drive
Bloomington, IN 47403
www.balboapress.com
1 (877) 407-4847

Because of the dynamic nature of the Internet, any web addresses or
links contained in this book may have changed since publication and
may no longer be valid. The views expressed in this work are solely those
of the author and do not necessarily reflect the views of the publisher,
and the publisher hereby disclaims any responsibility for them.

The author of this book does not dispense medical advice or prescribe the use
of any technique as a form of treatment for physical, emotional, or medical
problems without the advice of a physician, either directly or indirectly. The
intent of the author is only to offer information of a general nature to help
you in your quest for emotional and spiritual well-being. In the event you use
any of the information in this book for yourself, which is your constitutional
right, the author and the publisher assume no responsibility for your actions.

Printed in the United States of America.

ISBN: 978-1-4525-2366-8 (sc)
ISBN: 978-1-4525-2368-2 (hc)
ISBN: 978-1-4525-2367-5 (e)

Library of Congress Control Number: 2014918259

Balboa Press rev. date: 10/24/2014

To you Dear Reader,

Who understands the value of self-awareness and growth.

I dedicate this book to all of us gloriously
embracing the adventure of life.

INTRODUCTION

As soon as I released *Find Your Happy, an Inspirational Guide to Loving Life to its Fullest*, readers all over the world reached out to share the impact it had on them.

Many expressed their enthusiasm for the content and used it as a daily guide, often rereading it again and again. But the real gift was the impact this book had on people who reached happiness while leaving depression, fear and pain behind.

Find Your Happy helped people who suffered from depression, self-doubt and pain for years – even decades. This book in your hands, as well as *Find Your Happy*, is more than a self-help guide. It is a tool for recovery, providing hope and a path to freedom from pain.

Any recovery process requires a dedicated practice, which is why it became clear the next step was to transform *Find Your Happy* into a daily practice, using mantras, or daily meditations. I invite you to dive into this book *Find Your Happy Daily Mantras* with an open heart and self-compassion.

Whether you have read *Find Your Happy* or not, this book provides daily motivation to aid in your everlasting happiness. It is a tool for recovery from addictions, disease, pain, depression, anxiety and fear.

This book will help you along your journey and gently guide you to new awareness and inner peace.

Several years ago, I was diagnosed with clinical depression. At the time, I was also suffering from eating disorders and addicted to drugs. I hit rock bottom and my full surrender was the key to transformation. I turned my pain into purpose by sharing my journey of recovery. There is life after pain. It is possible. I am living proof.

Today I am happy, peaceful and living my life to the fullest.

I am so happy you choose to find your happy and are ready to transform your life from the inside out. The following pages serve as a 365-day practice to help turn happiness into a habit.

You are about to embark on a 365-day journey into wholeness, happiness and your authentic self. Inside I share my signature life coaching principals and the key to my own happiness.

Many people ask me how I overcame depression to live a happy and fulfilling life. Well, you are holding the instructions. The key to happiness is in the practice and I've put it into a handy guide for you to enjoy.

The moment you choose to pick up this book, the healing began. You can read this book in chronological order (one day at a time) or you can open to a random page and trust that is the message for you in the moment.

Feel free to open the book each morning and throughout the day to receive the guidance in an instant. Similar to an oracle deck ask a question or concern to the universe or your heart, then turn inward to be guided to a page. Trust that message you open up to is the one for you to receive.

This book was designed to be read one page a day. I encourage you to set time aside each day to make happiness your favorite habit.

My wish is for you to use this book as a daily inspiration, to help guide you to live your full potential.

No matter what, this book will take the *Find Your Happy* to new heights with added material, new tools and break through principals you can practice daily. Each day is setup to deliver motivation for you to live a happy, peaceful and fulfilling life.

Enjoy the adventure as you find your happy.

Love filled hugs,
Shannon Kaiser

I am brave and courageous with my heart.

I AM BRAVE AND COURAGEOUS WITH MY HEART.

If you have any doubts or concerns, now is the time to release them. You may not feel ready to step into the next phase of your life, but you are more prepared than you realize. Let your courageous heart guide you.

• • •

My heart is my compass for a happy life. If there is any area of my life I am unsatisfied with, now is the time for me to trust myself and my heart.

My heart will always lead me to the right solution to overcome all challenges. I am brave in my undertaking as I move forward with confidence. All of the fear I feel will be removed when I listen to the pulse of my dreams in my heart.

• • •

Where is my heart guiding me?

I AM ABUNDANT AND SECURE.

Now is the time to take care of your resources and focus on what you have. It will not serve you to focus on the lack. Giving time, money or energy to an organization you care about will help you feel more abundant and therefore create an abundant flow of resources to you. You are always safe and protected.

• • •

My worries and fears can sometimes get the best of me. But my truth knows I am always taken care of. The universe has an abundant supply of everything I desire. I am protected and safe and I allow myself to focus on the good instead of what is not working. I release all lack mentality and turn to the abundance apparent already. I feel safe in the moment and all my needs are always meet.

• • •

In what ways am I abundant?

I RELEASE ALL WORRY.
I CELEBRATE WHAT
COULD GO RIGHT.

Positive thinking is important for you right now. Any troubling, negative thoughts could prevent you from reaching your goals. Instead of worrying about what could go wrong, start to celebrate what could go right.

• • •

My worry does not serve me. It is like praying for what I don't want, and this hinders my ability to be happy. Instead of worry, I turn to trust. I know a plan is at play and I am being guided.

When I turn to my future self, I know everything always falls into place. If it is supposed to be part of my life plan, it will. I trust divine timing and allow my life to unfold naturally.

• • •

The worry I am willing to
release is_____?

ALL MY NEEDS ARE ALWAYS MET.

There is no need for you to stay in any situation that no longer serves you. If an area of your life feels strained because you don't understand how it could possibly work out, you can turn to trust. Plenty of possibilities are available to you when you are open to receiving.

• • •

I admit I sometimes get ahead of myself and become consumed with frustration. I release my need to know the outcome and align with my inner self.

I know I am taken care of and all my needs are met. When I fall into fear, I simply return to my true self by looking at all the things I do have.

• • •

What am I grateful for today?

ALL I DESIRE IS ON ITS WAY TO ME.

Now is a perfect time for you to rest and recover from all your hard work. Perhaps you have spent time worrying about the outcome or consumed with frustration because you have not reached your goal. In your efforts, your results are strained. Taking time to relax can help you become more productive and discover new ways to reach your goals.

• • •

As I work toward my dreams, I remove all frustration and jealousy. When I see other people who have what I desire, I repeat, "Thank you, universe, for showing me what is possible for me."

I send others love and light and know that my dreams matter. I find the joy in the journey of reaching my goals. The magic of living a fulfilling life is in celebrating my process as well as the outcome. The universe is guiding me. I trust the signs that lead to my big picture.

• • •

What person or situation have I been jealous off?
Repeat what I see and admire in them is on its way to me.

I AM OPEN AND WILLING TO LIVE MY LIFE IN NEW WAYS.

You may be in a situation that has not worked out as planned, but now is the time to try again. Closed doors will always lead to new opportunities for growth and expansion. Your power is not in how the situation has played out, but in how you proceed.

• • •

Setbacks in life can be surprising opportunities for growth. Although this time of my life may be uncertain, I trust my future self is guiding me. I am willing to see the silver lining and am open to living my life in refreshing new ways.

I believe everything happens for a reason and I am willing to see the big picture of all difficult situations. As I move through my life transitions, I release the old and welcome new ways of living. All is for my greatest good.

• • •

What new patterns and habits can I invite into my life?

THE UNIVERSE HAS A PLAN GREATER THAN MINE.

Have faith in your inner wisdom and trust the timing of your dreams. You may feel conflicted or unsure of your path, but today is the time to turn inward and trust the nudges coming to you. You are always being guided and the inspiration from within will lead you in the right direction.

• • •

I don't always get what I want, but I know I will always get what I truly need. I may feel stuck and at a standstill at times. But when I turn inward, I know all is in order.

I know I am being guided. When things don't go my way, I will turn to my inner knowing that things are actually falling into place. Nothing is ever out of order when it comes to my life plan. I see evidence of this in my past. Things have worked out in the long run. I can reflect for a gentle reminder that all is as it should be.

• • •

What in my past has worked out for the best?

EVERYTHING IS IN DIVINE ORDER.

Close your eyes and wish upon a star. The universe is working out a divine plan for you and all is in your favor. Feel hopeful and purposeful. Believe in your dreams as they will come true for you. In this moment, you may feel paused or stuck. This is only temporary, as readjusting is in process.

• • •

There is a sacred timing to everything in my life. I release any concern that I am not where I need to be. I have made no mistakes and where I am in this moment is perfect.

When I start to worry about missing opportunities or when fears from the past creep in, I place my hand on my heart and repeat, Everything is in divine order. I am right where I am supposed to be.

• • •

What concerns am I willing to release?

I AM SURROUNDED BY LOVE. I AM PROTECTED.

You are so much stronger than you give yourself credit for. You may feel alone and unsafe, but today is a reminder that you are always protected and surrounded by love. Infinite energy surrounds you and wants you to succeed. You are more than willing and capable to overcome any current challenges. Instead of powering your way through it, shower the situation with love.

• • •

The only thing keeping me from moving forward is my fear and recurring worry. The negative energy around me is not serving me, so I choose to release it and see the love surrounding me.

I surround the situations in my life that feel uncertain and unsafe with positivity. I let light in and I know I am always protected.

• • •

What area of my life do I feel unsafe and how can I let more love into this situation?

I TURN MY LACK INTO LOVE.

Devote your energy to what you want. Turn your attention to the loving presence within you instead of listening to your fear. The lack mentality you feel is a false belief sprung from insecurity. You can eliminate your concerns by returning to love.

• • •

I am aligned with my truth and that is love. When I feel overwhelmed because of life's demands, I back down and hide myself. This does not serve the world or me. Instead of allowing my fear to take over, I choose love by focusing on all that is well.

• • •

What areas of my life are going well?

I AM ALIGNED WITH MY TRUTH AND MY TRUTH IS LOVE.

Stretch your wings and prepare to soar. You have worked hard to get to where you are. And it will pay off. Align with your authentic self and all will be in right order. When you choose love, you will flourish.

• • •

When I fall into worry and insecure thoughts, I return to my true self. I am pure love and I align with my pure energy. Love is my truth and I embrace the good that is.

I have worked hard to get to where I am today and none of my efforts are in vain. I am aligned with the good which is my truth, divine love.

• • •

Where can I let more love in?

I SURRENDER.

Allow recent events in your life to be a wakeup call for some life changes. When you feel as though you have exhausted all options, know that surrender is in order. Surrendering is not giving up, but rather saying *I let go of the outcome and proceed forward without expectations*. This energy is infectious and will help you overcome any troubling situation.

• • •

I may not be where I think I need to be, but I know I am doing the best I can. I tried and gave it all I had. Although it feels like it wasn't enough, I know it was purposeful.

I let go of the outcome and surrender to what is. I cannot change the situation, but I can learn and grow from it.

• • •

Where can I surrender?

THE ONLY APPROVAL I NEED IS MY OWN.

You are far too hard on yourself. What others say about you or to you is only a reflection of their position in life. They bring insecurities, worries and their own fears to each conversation. Instead of taking on what they feel, align yourself with your truth. When you approve of your own decisions and choices, you will be free.

• • •

I release my need for others to accept and approve of me. Instead I turn my attention to my own desires and focus on why I am doing what I am doing. When I am aligned with my truth, I am confident, supported and alive.

My desires matter and I live them openly and with integrity. I approve of myself and my desires are in motion.

• • •

In what area of my life do I seek more confidence?
What action steps can I take to cultivate more approval for myself?

ABUNDANCE AND JOY
ARE MY BIRTHRIGHT.

There is no need for you to be in fear. Joy is natural to you. Stop holding onto negative and fearful thoughts. There is no need to worry as you were born to be happy. Instead of giving your attention to things that bother you, allow them to fall away. Harmony will soon come to you, as joy and abundance is your birthright.

• • •

I am not my worries or concerns. I am so much bigger than any dilemmas in my life. I choose to see the good in each situation and I focus my attention on all that is well. I am joyful and connected to my truth. Joy is my natural state of well-being and I align with it daily. I always have everything I need and happiness flows to me.

• • •

What does abundance mean to me?

OUT OF DIFFICULTIES GROW NEW BEGINNINGS. I TRUST THE PROCESS.

Recent events may have caused you to worry, but today is a reminder to focus your attention on new beginnings. What ended is no longer serving you in your life. It is safe to release all troubling situations.

You can use your imagination to solve the problem and create new approaches. You have everything you need to move into the next phase of your life. You are being guided and you are safe and protected.

• • •

I refuse to get caught up in my life dramas. Instead of holding onto the pain, I let it go with forgiveness and compassion. I step forward with confidence and trust my new beginning is appropriate for my big picture.

My life is important and I allow myself to be fully in the process. I release my past so I can be present for my future.

• • •

What am I holding onto and unwilling to let go of?

WHEN I FOLLOW MY PASSIONS MY PURPOSE IS REVEALED.

You might be trying too hard to find your purpose. If you are overthinking and struggling to find the answers, you could be blocking the answers from coming. Instead of thinking your way into your purpose, try to feel your way into it. Ask yourself what feels right as you explore new opportunities and ventures. Finding your purpose is a process that derives from your heart.

• • •

I am in the process and I trust my plan is being revealed to me. When I focus on what brings me joy, I live on purpose and this brings me clarity.

I align with what feels good and step away from limiting beliefs such as I have to have it figured out. My life is perfect the way it is and I am joyfully expressing myself.

• • •

What brings me the most joy today?

WHEN I CLEAN UP MY THOUGHTS, I CLEAN UP MY LIFE.

Just like a magnet that attracts its likeness, the laws of the universe state your thoughts create your reality. If you are dissatisfied with an area of your life, it is essential you take responsibility and consider your recent and current thoughts. When you clean up your thoughts, you clean up your life. You attract to you that which occurs.

• • •

I am accountable for all that I experience. I choose loving, kind and supportive thoughts, which help align me with my truth. I solve all situations with love. My current reality is a result of my previous thoughts. If I want to change my situation, I start by changing my thoughts about it. I release the negative hold of fear and align with my truth and love. I attract good things to me.

• • •

Where can I take responsibility for my outcome?

EVERYTHING I NEED
IS INSIDE OF ME.

You may worry you don't have what you need to get to where you want to go. But today is a reminder you have everything you will ever need to reach your goals. Your future is unfolding in the present moment and it is essential you hold positive thoughts. You are more capable and willing than you give yourself credit for. Instead of focusing on how it can't work, turn your attention to opportunities in front of you. When you are open to receiving guidance, there are plenty of ways to reach your desired outcome.

• • •

I am strong, capable and focused. I release my need to have it all figured out and go inward to reveal the best path forward. I am always being guided to learn, grow and trust more. Today, I align with my truth, the desires from my heart. I take one step at a time and the path is revealed to me. I always have what I need to get to where I want to go. I learn the way on the way.

• • •

Where can I give myself more credit for a job well done?

I BELIEVE IN THE GOOD OF MANKIND.

For the next two weeks, turn your attention inward and stop looking outside to the media and news for current events. Life is happening all around you, but when you turn to negative coverage, it projects a one-sided view. The world is a kind and loving place and when you can align with love, you will see evidence of this.

• • •

I release my attention on the negative current events and focus on the qualities of mankind that are good. I see beauty in people and I smile with joy.
I give people the benefit of the doubt and release harsh judgment and criticism. I know everyone is doing the best they can and together we can all choose love and peace.

• • •

What qualities of mankind do I love?

WHAT I SEEK IS ON
ITS WAY TO ME.

At any given moment, you have a choice. You can focus on what is not yet here or you can turn your attention to what is working in your life. Focus actively on the good qualities of your life and you will begin to see evidence of your desires in motion. What you desire also desires you. So it is important to hold faith that what you want is on its way, because it is.

• • •

I align with my highest good and all I desire is on its way to me. What I seek is seeking me. Even though I cannot see evidence of my outcome, I hold faith I will get what I need at the right time for me. My desires are in full bloom and I hold faith they will come true soon.

• • •

How can I focus more on what is working instead of what is not?

THERE IS A PURPOSE TO MY PAIN.

You may feel challenged by your current situation, but today is a reminder that you are being groomed for great things. Although your recent path may have been difficult, you will overcome these troubling times. Through life's difficulties is an opportunity for great expansion and wonderful growth. Trust you are on a path of understanding and this pain will soon make sense. Hold the faith.

• • •

I am bigger than anything that happens to me. I rise above all pain to see my strength. I am growing into the person I want to become. I release all troubling situations and I know this too shall pass.

• • •

What challenges from my past can I celebrate overcoming?

THERE ARE NO WRONG DECISIONS. I GROW FROM ALL MY CHOICES.

If you only do what you are comfortable with, you will never grow. The choices you have made were not in vain. They have led you to a greater understanding of self and your place in the world. Instead of regretting your past, look at the benefits of what became of each outcome.

• • •

I am a perfect example of growing from my life experience. I trust everything is falling into place and my past has helped me become who I am supposed to be. I forgive myself and shine my light forward. I grow from all my choices.

• • •

What have I learned from a choice I regret?

I AM NOT ALONE.

Although you may feel alone, you are never truly by yourself. Your heart, support system, guides, higher power and higher self are always with you, gently guiding you to peace and understanding. If you feel lonely, turn your focus to the love around you. You are protected and cared for, now and always.

• • •

I am never truly alone. I may feel lonely, but I know I am surrounded by love. I trust the silence as it allows me to go inward to express my truth from my heart. I am safe, protected and secure. I am never alone.

• • •

Who can I reach out to for companionship?

MY STRESS IS TRYING TO TELL ME SOMETHING.

You may be overwhelmed and working too hard. If you feel stressed, this is an indication of imbalance and your life is not flowing. Instead of trying to get it all done and work hard to make something happen, consider a more playful, fun approach. When you add joy to your routine, your stress levels go down.

• • •

I remove all unnecessary worry and tasks from my life. I choose to focus on adding more playful energy to my stressful situations. This helps me get out of my own way so I can be more productive and playful.

• • •

Where can I add more play into my life?

REGARDLESS OF THE OUTCOME, I AM TAKEN CARE OF.

You need not worry about the resolution of the current situation. Instead of trying to solve the problem with sheer force, trust you will get exactly what you need. No matter the outcome to the uncertain situation, you are taken care of.

• • •

All of my needs are met. I am full of love and my attention is on the present moment. For in this moment, I have everything I need and I am secure. No matter what the outcome, I know it will be for my greater good.

• • •

What negative belief can you let go of
regarding an uncertain situation?

I CELEBRATE LIFE'S LITTLE VICTORIES.

Are you worrying too much? If so, you are probably focused on the outcome instead of enjoying the process. If you were to stop and reflect, you would see how extraordinary you truly are and how far you have already come. Celebrate where you are today, for you are brilliantly beautiful in this moment. You are doing a great job.

• • •

I am proud of how far I have come. I celebrate my life and all of the little victories along the way. I have goals I am working toward but I am happy to be where I am. I accept myself and embrace the process fully.

• • •

What little victories am I proud of?

NEEDING SOMEONE IS NOT A WEAKNESS. IT IS AN ACT OF SELF-LOVE.

Relying on someone else is not a weakness. You have been strong for so long and there is no need to have your guard up. Instead of protecting your heart, consider a more vulnerable approach and let love in. By showing someone you need them, you respect yourself more.

• • •

It is safe to show the real me. I need help and support and I am open to receiving this support from loved ones. I show up for myself when I allow myself to need others. I am strong and independent, but needing someone is essential for my well-being. I let others in.

• • •

Where can I ask for help and who can I let in?

MY WRONG TURNS PUT ME ON THE RIGHT PATH.

It may feel like some events in your life have come to a standstill, but it is time for reevaluation. What may feel like a wrong turn could be stirring you in the right direction. There are no wrong turns, only opportunities for growth. Trust this process and learn from your past mistakes.

• • •

I am exactly where I need to be in my life. I know I am being divinely led to a higher purpose and I trust the plan. I may feel off track, but when I return to my heart, it reveals the right way. All is in right order for me and all is well.

• • •

What can I forgive myself for?

THE PRESENT MOMENT IS ALL THAT MATTERS.

You may feel overwhelmed with specific situations and outcomes in your life. Now is not the time to worry or try to control the outcome. Look at where you are holding onto expectations and release them. When you feel overwhelmed by life's circumstances, know fearing for the future will not serve you. All we have is this moment, so turn your attention to the now, and the fear will subside.

• • •

I understand some things are out of my control and I am okay with that. I release all fear from my past and anxiety for the future. Instead, I return to the moment and know that things are always as they should be.

• • •

What expectations am I ready to release?

CLUTTER IS A BYPRODUCT OF INDECISION. I REMOVE ALL EXTRA STUFF FROM MY LIFE.

If you are overwhelmed with a situation, consider looking at the clutter in your life. Everything is connected and clutter in your home is a byproduct of indecision.

Clutter can be physical or emotional. Now is the time to remove all extra stuff and welcome in new energy that is aligned with your truth.

• • •

My thoughts are pure, my energy is light and I am clutter free. I take time to remove everything that no longer serves me. This includes people, products, ideas and beliefs. By releasing what no longer works, I make room for what does.

• • •

What can I remove from my life?

NOTHING EVER HAPPENS THAT ISN'T SUPPOSED TO.

You may get ahead of yourself and worry if things are working out the way they are supposed to. When you turn your attention inward, you will see everything is always falling into place. Turn your lack to love by trusting the process of your life.

• • •

I am aligned with my inner knowing and truth. I know everything in my life is part of a bigger plan and there are no wrong turns. I release any false beliefs based in fear and accept my truth, which is to honor the process that unfolds in front of me. All is in right order.

• • •

How can I be more in the process of my life?

I RELEASE MY NEED
TO GET THERE.

Life is not a race. There is no final destination for you to arrive at. Each goal you create is part of a bigger life plan and process. Instead of focusing so much on the outcome, this is a gentle reminder to have more fun in the journey. The process is part of the goal, and it is where the magic can happen. You will look back one day and realize the little things were the real, tangible parts of your life. So enjoy the journey just as much as the destination.

• • •

I am in the process of my life and allow it to be what it is. I give up my need to manipulate my outcome or force myself to get there. Instead, I have fun along the way and play in the journey.

• • •

What outcome have I been holding onto?

IT'S NOT NAÏVE TO PUT A POSITIVE SPIN ON EVERYTHING.

You may have been taught that thinking positive is naïve and unrealistic. But putting a positive spin on all situations will help you see the big picture. There is a silver lining to everything, and it is up to you to see it. Believe in your big picture as all is connected and in right order.

• • •

I am guided by love, which allows me to focus forward with positive thoughts. I stand with courage and conviction that a big picture is at play. I trust my future self and I am aligned with love.

• • •

Where can I be more positive?

I RESPECT EXPIRATION DATES.

Everyone has moments of insecurity and fear. Sometimes these fears stem from insecurities and worries about the unknown. You may be holding onto a situation that is supposed to end. If you feel as though you are putting an enormous amount of energy into a situation, person or thing and not getting a solid return, it may be time to release it.

• • •

I trust the divine timing to all situations in my life. I openly accept new opportunities and release what no longer serves me. I know everything in my life is an opportunity for expansion and growth. I let go of relationships, places and jobs ready to end. I welcome in new opportunities for change.

• • •

What am I holding on to that I can let go of?

I RELEASE MY FEAR OF OPENING UP TO NEW PEOPLE. I LET LOVE IN.

It may be difficult to open up to new people. But your future self is guiding you and you are protected in each new experience. When we approach new people and situations, we can feel timid or afraid. But this is based on insecurity and lack. Instead of wondering what others will think of you, trust yourself and let love in. They will love you when you show your true self.

• • •

The world needs me as I am. When I show my true self, I receive an honest echo reflected back. I am not afraid of looking others in the eye and showing them my authentic nature. I belong in this world and am perfect as I am. I let love in.

• • •

Where can I show more of my true self?

I ALLOW LOVE AND LIGHT INTO MY LIFE.

You have an original ingenuity about you. Now is the time to accept your full self and show your real nature. You may have felt reserved or hesitant to show your true colors, but when you allow more love into your life, you feel more loved. The world wants and needs you as you are. Shine bright and go forward with confidence, love and clarity.

• • •

I am surrounded by love and I am always cared for. I choose to focus all my efforts on loving acts with self-compassion as my guide. I let love into my life and I accept it openly and fully.

• • •

What area of my life can I allow more love in?

I allow love and
light into my life.

WHEN I FOLLOW MY HEART I AM ABUNDANT, SUCCESSFUL, AND FREE.

You are only trapped by the thoughts in your mind. Drop to your heart for more clarity. Perhaps you worry about all your needs being met. Today is a day to remember that you are always abundant and successful. All of your past decisions have lead you to where you are today. By celebrating the present moment you will feel the freedom within. Your heart is always speaking to you, now is the time to listen.

• • •

I turn inward to listen to my heart. I trust the guidance from within. I remove all external critics and release the need to fit in. When I follow my heart all falls into place. I am free.

• • •

In what ways can I cultivate more freedom in my life?

I LET GO OF WHAT I CAN'T CHANGE.

The need to control your environment might be strong. You may feel out of sorts when things don't go your way. Today is an opportunity for you to practice letting go. You always have a choice. You can try to change what you are unwilling to accept. But at some point, you will see letting go of what you can't change is real acceptance.

• • •

I release my control on things I cannot accept. Instead of trying to force things to go a certain way, I trust the universe is working on my behalf. I see everything in life has its own time and place, and I allow all to be as it is. I let go.

• • •

What can I let go of that I cannot change?

FORGIVENESS ISN'T ABOUT FREEING ME FROM MY PAST. IT IS ABOUT OPENING UP MY FUTURE.

Be honest with yourself and look at relationships where you are harboring resentment. Perhaps you have tried to forgive, but struggled to release the situation from your life. Maybe you feel it is unspiritual to be angry, so you try to pretend everything is okay. Allow yourself to feel the feelings. This will let them move through you and release them for good. Then forgiveness can set in.

• • •

I give myself permission to feel my feelings. I allow them to move through me. I look at all areas of my life and clean out emotional clutter by releasing resentment. My actions are guided with love. I am letting go of my past so I can free myself up to new opportunities in my future. I forgive.

• • •

Who can I forgive today?

MY FAMILY MATTERS. I SHOW THEM MY LOVE AND APPRECIATION.

Your family may cause you distress, but they often mean well. You may feel unsupported in your life. But when you show love and appreciation to others, you will get the support you need. Instead of focusing on how your family has wronged you, look at the lessons you learned from them.

Perhaps you have more self-love, more gratitude or more clarity. Our family is our biggest opportunity for growth. Let your family be your guide to a greater understanding of yourself.

• • •

I know my family didn't mean to cause me harm. They may say things that bring up stuff for me, but I release my attachment of needing their approval. I honor myself by being true to myself. Eventually, my family will see me for who I am and, in the meantime, I show my appreciation with loving allowance for them to be as they are.

• • •

What family member can I send love and light to right now?

I DON'T TAKE MYSELF TOO SERIOUSLY. I SEE THE LIGHTHEARTEDNESS IN THIS MOMENT.

Life can be difficult and it is even harder when you take everything seriously. Today's opportunity is to bring more joy into this moment. Seriousness has its own time and place, but in the situation causing you the most distress, consider bringing in more lighthearted energy. This will give way to new opportunities to solve the problem.

• • •

I smile more and let light in. I maybe taking myself too seriously, which does not serve me. Instead of powering my way through this troubling situation, I smile and invite more lighthearted energy into my life. I am happy and free.

• • •

Where can I lighten up?

EVERYTHING'S GOING TO BE ALL RIGHT. IT ALWAYS WORKS OUT IN THE END.

If you look back on your life, you may see proof that everything always works out in the end. If you are in a situation causing you extreme stress, recognize it is not the end. Dive into the experience and you will come out on the other side with grace and ease.

• • •

I am worry-free and supported by my higher self. I choose to see all situations as opportunities for expansive growth. I know things are falling into place. And everything always works out in the end. I trust my internal guidance as I move forward.

• • •

What past experiences have worked out in my favor?

LIFE IS ABOUT DETOURS. I TAKE THE ROAD LESS TRAVELED AND EMBRACE THE UNKNOWN.

You may feel as though your life is off track, but you are more on track than you have ever been. Your life is a creative exploration of arriving at your true self. Trust the process and be open to glorious detours. The road in front of you is paved by your own adventure. Embrace the unknown.

• • •

I am open to taking new paths to solve old problems. I am fearless. I face forward with confidence and jump into my life with wide open arms. My heart is the compass. I take detours and know they lead me to a greater awareness of my place in this world. My life is an adventure I navigate with love.

• • •

How can I step out of my comfort zone today?

I REEVALUATE AND REVIEW MY LIFE OFTEN. IT'S OKAY TO GO IN A DIFFERENT DIRECTION.

You may be on autopilot in certain areas of your life. Although this can serve you in the long run, it is necessary to take stock and reevaluate often. Perhaps an area of your life has become stale or boring. Look deeper to see what the disenchantment may be about.

• • •

It is okay to go in a new direction. My life is a constant, every-changing experience and what once worked for me may no longer be a good fit. I give myself time to reevaluate and sort out any area that no longer brings me joy. I release all that no longer serves me.

• • •

What area of my life have I become disenchanted with and what is that trying to tell me?

I TRUST MY INTUITION.

Your inner guidance system is an intricate orchestra of love and passion. When you tune into your own wisdom, you will never fail. Trust yourself, as you know yourself on a soul level, deeper than anyone else in the world. Now is the time to listen deeply to the voice within. It is leading you to where you truly long to go.

• • •

I trust myself. My inner voice is always speaking to me and it feels expansive. I align with my true intuition, which is light filled and joyful. My purpose is to follow my heart and I trust the voice within. My intuition is my best mentor forward. I listen to its honest reflection of my truth.

• • •

What has my intuition been trying to tell me?

I AM NOT DAMAGED OR WOUNDED. THERE IS NOTHING WRONG WITH ME.

The situations from your past have not damaged you. They have taught you lessons about life and your true awareness of self. Your current circumstances are not a result of you being unfixable. You are stronger and more capable then you give yourself credit for. Dive forward with confidence and whole heart love.

• • •

I am a warrior of my past. I am an overcomer and survivor of all that life has thrown at me. I am not damaged. There is nothing to fix. I am a perfect child of the universe and I am full of love. I shine my light forward with confidence and courage. I matter. I am whole.

• • •

Where do I feel broken? What steps will I
take to release this internal pain?

ANYTHING I GIVE MY ATTENTION TO WILL FLOURISH AND GROW.

Pay attention to where you focus your thoughts. What you see is a result of where you have been putting your emotional energy. If there is an area of your life you are dissatisfied with, look back to your recent and current thoughts about that situation. Turn your focus to what you want, and watch it flourish and grow.

• • •

I am responsible for all I experience. I always align with my loving light and focus on what I want with joy and ease. I release all worry and spend my time creating my joy-filled reality. When I focus on what I want, it flourishes and comes to me.

• • •

What area of my life can I give more loving attention to?

I DANCE THROUGH LIFE WITH GRACE AND EFFORTLESS EASE.

The journey of your life is a long, fascinating dance. When you dive into the rhythms of your life and let situations flow, you are graceful and connected to your spirit. Trust the dance is the journey and the rhythm of your heart is what will free you. Enjoy the dance.

• • •

My life is a fun experience full of peace and joy. I dance my way through each experience and new chapter of my life. I know there is a time for everything, and I glide gracefully through each phase. I am light on my feet. I am free, expansive and graceful.

• • •

Create a "Found My Happy" playlist.
What dance songs will I put on it?

I THINK FROM MY HEART.

Your rational mind works extra hard throughout your life. It may analyze everything and try yourself in order to make smart, calculated moves forward. But in the past, it may have kept you in situations that no longer served you.

Now is the time to think from your heart. You may be used to feeling with your heart and trusting the guidance, but thinking with you heart means aligning your head and heart into one. Your ego mind need not be separate. Your fear can turn into love when you think from your heart.

• • •

My heart has guidance for me, and I trust the process it reveals. I think with my heart as it shows me the correct next action. I am always safe and protected because my head and heart are aligned.

• • •

How can I align my head and heart to help me
move through my current situation?

IT IS OKAY TO CHANGE MY MIND.

You need not stay in any situation that causes you pain. At any given moment, you have the power and choice to change your mind. If an area of your life is bringing you down, consider changing your mind.

Your life is an ever-expansive journey and changing your mind is part of the big picture. Instead of resisting change or holding onto the old, free yourself up from the emotional confines by changing your mind.

• • •

I am comfortable with my choices and position in life. I change my mind with confidence and know I am being guided to new opportunities. When I quiet my fear-based voice, I can feel my truth from my heart. I am guided into new directions and it is safe to change my mind.

• • •

Where can I change my mind?

I AM IN LOVE WITH THE PROCESS. I LOOK FORWARD TO LEARNING NEW THINGS AS I GROW.

Slow down. You may be too focused on the outcome. When you can add more love into this moment, you will embrace the process more. Instead of racing to meet your goal, savor the sweet moments along the way. Through the process, you become who you are meant to be. Allow yourself to be more present in the journey, which will help you grow.

• • •

I am in no rush. I simply savor the sweet moments of my life and trust the divine unfolding of everything in its right time and place. I look forward to learning new things as I grow more into my best self.

• • •

What am I learning on the way to reaching my goal?

MY BELIEFS DO NOT DEFINE ME. I AM WILLING TO SEE OTHER PERSPECTIVES WITHOUT JUDGMENT.

You may get frustrated because others don't see things the way you do. Let go of the need to prove others right. Instead, see the diversity of life as a gift. Everyone is entitled to his or her own beliefs and opinions, including you. But do not mistake your views as a definition of who you are. You are so much more than your own beliefs, so consider a more open-minded approach to life as you move forward.

• • •

I am aligned with my inner light and my light is truth. I do not have a need to prove others right. They have opinions and beliefs that help color the contrast of the world. There is no wrong or right. We all belong.

Instead of defining myself or judging others by my opinions, I see us all as love and light. We are all connected by our diverse thoughts and ideals.

• • •

"Would I rather be right or happy?"
– ACIM

MY INNER CHILD
WANTS TO PLAY.

Most of your energy has been consumed with life's demands and adult responsibilities. But there is a more playful approach to life and that approach is already within you.

Your inner child has been with you all along, but has felt pushed aside. Your inner child is the true you, the one who is playful, compassionate, curious and full of love. Return to your true self and allow your inner child to come out and play.

• • •

I turn inward and allow my inner child to come forth. My joy-filled, expressive self deserves to be heard. My inner child has a message for me and I listen to the wisdom. Each day, I return to my true self by allowing my inner child to come out and play.

• • •

What did I love to do as a child that I can do today?

NOTHING IS AS IT SEEMS.

Your attention is on what you think you see, but your true self knows nothing is as it seems. The situation you perceive to be troubling could have a deeper message for you. Look closely at the stories you are telling yourself around the experience and consider other options available. Nothing is ever as it seems.

• • •

I know the universe is working behind the scenes in all situations in my life. When I turn my attention to my higher self, I can see this troubling situation is not what it seems. I trust the unfolding of my life and see that nothing is really ever as it seems.

• • •

Where have I thought one thing in the past but
it turned out as something different?

DIFFICULT SITUATIONS LEAD TO DIVINE SOLUTIONS.

Your life is paved with uncertain situations and rough patches, but when you turn your attention to the solutions, you will be divinely led. All difficult paths are opportunities for you to dive inward and see the true lesson. Each difficult experience will lead you to divine awareness and solutions.

• • •

I am in the journey of my life and I embrace each moment fully. Each difficult experience is a pathway to greatness within me. I see the divine solutions available in each moment. All setbacks are really growth and part of my over-arching life plan.

• • •

How can I view a troubling situation in my life in a new way?

I WITNESS SITUATIONS WITHOUT JUDGMENT.

When you judge situations, people and experiences, you prevent yourself from being present in your life. Judgment is a stand-in for lack of love. Instead of observing situations with a need to fix, solve or prove others wrong, consider a more compassionate approach. You can do this by stepping back and witnessing your life as if you are watching it on a movie screen. This allows you to see the big picture.

• • •

I am free of judgment and self-blame. I watch all situations in my life without a need to criticize, fix or blame. I am accountable for what I see, but I do not take it personally. I am free of all judgment and witness all situations with love.

• • •

What situation have I recently been overcritical about?
How can I send more love to this experience?

I AM HURTING AND THAT IS OKAY.

You need not hide your pain, nor do you need to push it away. Feeling hurt is part of living a balanced life. You may be on a spiritual path and feel as if you shouldn't be hurting or in pain. But this couldn't be further form the truth. True self-awareness comes from embracing all emotions as they come up.

Allow yourself to be in the pain as you feel it. It will remove itself from your life. Be kind to yourself. It takes time to heal. There is no expiration date on healing. Time will give you what you need.

• • •

I am hurting but that is part of the process of healing. It is okay to feel these emotions. I choose to dive into this pain, rather than numbing myself or running away. My pain has a message for me and I can learn from this experience. I embrace all of life's experiences and feel them fully.

• • •

Where have I blocked myself from feeling?

I SURRENDER ALL EXPECTATIONS.

You may focus too much on the outcome. When you care about something, you put your whole heart into it. There is nothing wrong with being passionate, but be careful not to energetically strain the outcome.

When you focus too much on how things will play out, you do not trust divine resolution. Instead of manipulating your energy and putting it in such strain, surrender your expectations by trusting all is in right order.

• • •

I am connected to my true self and know all is in perfect order. I have goals and deep desires, but they will be manifested in their own right time and place. I release my need to have things when and how I want, and I turn my trust to the universe. I always get what I need, when I need it. I surrender.

• • •

Where have I been focusing too much on the outcome?

I WAIT FOR THE RIGHT TIME.

Your life is unfolding perfectly, as planned. Fate and freewill are balanced and you are living it in this moment. If you want something but are unsure of the next right action, consider that the universe will guide you when the time is right.

If it feels forced to move forward, it is. It is not yet time. You will get clarity in the pause. Take time to review your plan and allow the universe to show you the right time.

• • •

I align with my heart and I trust the universe's plan. All things unfold in their right time and place. I am living my truth by being powerful in the pause. I only take action when I feel pulled from my heart. I wait for the right time and when it feels right.

• • •

Where in my life do I feel forced to take action?
I will consider a steadier pace and wait for my heart's guidance.

I AM WHERE I AM — NOT WHERE I THINK I SHOULD BE.

You may feel rushed or in a hurry to get to the next phase of your life. This is preventing you from getting there. Whether you are trying to lose weight, meet a soul mate, or get clarity around your life purpose, when you focus on being there, you miss being here. When you can fully accept where you are, you will get where you want to go much faster. Be present. It will give you what you want.

• • •

I am connected to my loving light and am present in this moment. I let go of all forced actions and stop trying so hard to get to there. Instead, I accept fully where I am today. I am okay with this moment and accept my place in my life.

• • •

What current situation in my life have I been resisting?

I AM LIVING PROOF OF ALL THAT IS POSSIBLE.

There is nothing you can't handle. You are strong and capable of moving forward though all situations in your life. You have been through so much and proven you are a survivor. Even if things are not perfect in your life, you can tap into a sense of peace within you. You are a miracle and your life is a gift.

• • •

I am surrounded by love and I am a survivor. I have overcome challenging situations, which have led me to a new approach to life. I am living proof miracles happen. I am a gift to the world.

• • •

In what ways can I appreciate myself more?

I SWEAT EVERY DAY.

Taking time to move your body will benefit you right now. You may feel static in an area of your life, but exercise and movement will help bring more life and energy into the situation.

When you take care of yourself, you shine from the inside out. When you focus on joy-filled activities that stretch your body and mind, you will be more productive and healthy. You honor yourself by celebrating yourself.

• • •

I am connected to my body and I choose activities that bring me joy. I know exercise is healthy for my overall well-being. My spirit flourishes when I take care of my body. I am healthy. I sweat every day.

• • •

What exercise can I do that brings me joy?

GRATITUDE IS THE LIFE FORCE OF EVERYTHING.

You may be focusing too much on what you don't have and what is not working. By turning your focus to gratitude, you will open up new opportunities. Being thankful is the life force for all you truly desire. Your path will become less strained when you turn your energy to love and gratitude.

• • •

I am thankful for all I am and all I have. My life is a perfect reflection of all I desire and things I want flow to me naturally. My life is in perfect balance as I turn my attention to what I appreciate most.

• • •

In what area of my life can I be more thankful?

I HAVE THE COURAGE
TO BE IMPERFECT.

You are perfect as you are. Your need to gain others approval stems from an inner drive to be seen and noticed for who you really are. When you show up courageously as your true self, you will get all you truly long for. The imperfections you hide out of fear of judgment are actually qualities others will adore. Give yourself permission to be the real you.

• • •

I am perfect in my imperfections. They help me be more real and relatable. I embrace all aspects of myself, including the areas of my character I try to hide. I know when I show my true self, I will be loved and respected. I have the courage to be the real me.

• • •

What flaw that I hide from others can I reveal?

THE WORST IS BEHIND ME.

Continue to forge forward. You are coming into a time of your own and the worst is now behind you. You have made great strides to overcome adversity and challenges. You can rest assured all your hard work will pay off. Now you will be rewarded.

• • •

I am strong and powerful. I have worked hard to get to where I am today. The worst is now behind me and I can celebrate my efforts. I gracefully move forward with confidence as all of my right actions are now rewarded.

• • •

Where can I celebrate a job well done?

I AM AWARE OF THE BIG PICTURE.

Now is a perfect time to create a blueprint for your future. You can look at all situations as long-term solutions. Any hiccups along the way will be sorted out with attention on the big picture.

Your long-term success is more important than the short-term benchmarks. So there is no need to get down on yourself for not being where you think you should be. Instead, put your energy into full force ahead.

• • •

I am connected to my big picture. I take action everyday that leads to my ultimate goal. I know I am being guided and my big picture is my compass for success. When I feel astray, I remind myself that my life is unfolding and these small setbacks are opportunity for realignment. I focus forward and align with my big picture.

• • •

What long-term success am I working to create?

I AM VIBRANT AND IN PICTURE PERFECT HEALTH.

A healthy lifestyle starts with a healthy mindset. Feeling vibrant from the inside out will help you feel more balanced in all areas of your life. When you focus your energy on good vibes, you will feel connected to your true self. You are always healthy and vibrant when you shine your light. Instead of focusing on the trouble areas of your body or diet, use this time to cultivate new habits that help you feel healthy.

• • •

I am healthy and connected to my body. I care about what I put in my body and I make conscious choices to aid in my healthy energy. I choose foods that make me feel alive and healthy. I am healed from all sickness and disease. My body is a beacon of true energy and pure light. I am love. I am healthy.

• • •

What healthier habits can I start?

IT ISN'T WHAT I HAVE THAT MATTERS. IT IS WHAT I DO WITH WHAT I HAVE.

You might be focusing too much on lack and what you don't have. But you have everything you need inside of you to get to where you want to go. You have been given a unique set of gifts and talents that only you can bring forward. Stop spending so much time on what you don't have and start to embrace and use what you do.

• • •

I am connected to my true self. I have a unique power in me that can help me with everything I need in life. I spend my time honoring my unique self and use my talents wisely. I understand it is not how the cards fall that matters, but how I proceed forward with what I have been dealt.

• • •

What can I do with my current limitations?

MY DREAMS WILL ONLY SUCCEED WHEN I TAKE A CHANCE ON THEM.

Your dreams are important and they come to you for a reason. When you are inspired, you should take action. Look at a recent dream of yours that manifested into reality. It took courage and dedication but you did it. Give yourself the recognition you deserve and find it in you to do this again. Your future self is counting on you to take a chance on your dreams. You won't regret it.

• • •

I am attracted to my future as my dreams are in full focus. I am a success and living proof of all that is possible. I choose to follow my heart in every moment, as I move forward with courage and determination. My dreams matter. I give them respect by fearlessly moving forward.

• • •

What dream have I ignored, but it keeps coming back to mind? What action step can I take to move this dream forward?

IT'S THIS OR SOMETHING BETTER.

You may have experienced what seems like a setback or temporary pause. Instead of looking at the situation as a loss, consider you are being protected and groomed for something much better for you. Remember, rejection is protection, so you are not actually at a loss. Instead turn all your energy into what you truly want to feel and align with that energy. What you desire will come to you in the right form at the right time.

• • •

I am no longer determined to reach my goal in the means I thought best. I see multiple ways to get what I want and I am open to the universe guiding me to the right next action. I am connected to my big picture and it is this or something better.

• • •

What situation in my life turned out to
be a giant blessing in disguise?

I BELIEVE IN WHAT I CAN'T SEE.

Miracles are happening around you in every moment. Just because you can't always see the fruits of your labor does not mean your efforts are in vain. Turn your focus to what you believe in and focus forward with confidence.

Just because you can't always see situation playing out the way you hope does not mean it is time to give up. Keep focusing forward and believe in what you cannot yet see. It will soon manifest into your life and all your energy will pay off.

• • •

I stand behind my dreams and believe in them with all my heart. I may not see the outcome in my current reality, but I know it exists and is on its way to me. I visualize my success and see myself actively achieving my desires. I believe and I will achieve.

• • •

What can't I see that I believe in?

FEAR OF THE UNKNOWN IS A BYPRODUCT OF SETTLING. I DON'T SETTLE.

If you spend a lot of your time focusing on fears associated with the unknown, now is the time to release them. Perhaps you are allowing yourself to settle. You deserve more in your life and you can move away from this fear-based thought pattern by aligning with your true worth.

• • •

I am connected to my future by moving gracefully through the unknown. I understand every step of my journey leads me to a deeper understanding of my honest self. I release all worry connected to the unknown, for I am safe and I am being guided.

• • •

Where have I been settling? And what actions step can I take to raise my standards?

My soul is rooting for me.

Day No. 73

MY SOUL IS ROOTING FOR ME.

You may be putting too many hours into a specific situation. It is necessary to recalibrate, rebalance and refocus your attention, possible into a new direction. Your soul is rooting for you and will guide you to take the next right action. When you turn inward and ask your heart what it needs, your soul will guide you to what you truly want.

• • •

I have worked hard to get to where I am, and for today that is enough. I celebrate all of my hard work and know I am being guided. My soul is rooting for me. I can make it through this tough time. My troubles disappear as I align to my true heart's purpose. I am connected to my soul and I know it is celebrating my successes.

• • •

What right next action am I being guided to take?

I FEEL MY FEAR AND DO IT ANYWAY.

Your fear is speaking to you and it is an indicator of what you need to do. When the fear is loud and debilitating, you can be certain it is trying to show you something. Instead of being paralyzed by your fear, look deep into it and see what it is trying to show you. When you step through the fear, you will see it was a guidance system leaning you into your true self. Feel your fear and, instead of turning away, go through it.

• • •

I feel my fear and move through it with graceful attention. I see my fear can lead me into new awareness of my authentic self. When my fear gets loud, it is an indication of what is most important to me. By stepping though my fear, I am touched with love and purpose. I step courageously into the next chapter of my life.

• • •

What is my fear trying to tell me?

MY LONELINESS IS NOT AN INVITATION TO SETTLE.

You may feel lonely but this does not mean you are alone. Your loneliness can be a teacher of greater understanding of yourself and your true needs. Put your attention on what you desire, which will cultivate a deep awareness within. Instead of focusing on the lack or what is not available to you, give yourself the love you desire. The love you seek will soon find you.

• • •

I am never truly alone. I may feel lonely, but I allow myself to feel this emotion. When I feel it, it moves through me and I can release it. My loneliness is not an invitation to settle. I deserve respect and align my life to my values. The love I deserve is on its way to me, but I first must give it to myself.

• • •

What relationships have I settled in and what steps can I take to raise my worth?

I AM KIND TO MYSELF. I KNOW I AM DOING THE BEST I CAN.

Everything you have ever done has been from a need to want or give more love. And love is never wrong. Instead of allowing your inner critic to run the show, treat yourself with kindness and self-respect. You are doing a tremendous job and for today it is enough.

• • •

I take loving action and move forward in life with self-compassion and kindness. My life is unfolding as it is supposed to and nothing I have ever done or said is wrong. Every choice has led me to where I am today. I am doing the best I can and that is enough.

• • •

In what ways can I be kinder to myself?

I ENTHUSIASTICALLY PURSUE MY INNOVATIVE IDEAS.

Inspiration comes to you because you are the best person to bring it into the world. When you have a dream that hits your heart, it is your mission to see it to life. Enthusiastically jump into the process and watch your ideas flourish.

• • •

I am full of possibilities and open to new ideas that flow to me. I trust the guidance I receive and take action steps forward. My ideas are important and the steps I take today will cultivate a strong foundation for my future. I am divinely led to new adventures and opportunity.

• • •

What ideas have come to me that I can action forward?

I CAN TRY AGAIN.

You may be in a situation that has not worked out the way you wanted. You can always try again. Perseverance is essential as you step forward into the next phase of your life. The past is not a failure but an opportunity for learning. As you examine what didn't work, you will get clarity about what does work. Keep going and try again.

• • •

I am in integrity and connected to my truth. I know my past situation is part of my bigger picture. Nothing is wasted or out of place. I turn inward to observe all my experiences and study them with an objective eye. As I learn what doesn't work, I become clearer about what does. I can always try again.

• • •

What have I given up on that still wants to be pursued?

I DON'T NEED A REASON TO HELP OTHERS.

You might think it is important to help others because it makes you a good person. Although this is true, ask yourself if you help others because it seems like the right thing to do? When you help those in need because of outside influences, it hinders your ability to truly help. Instead of focusing on what others need from you, or what looks right to others, give to others for no reason.

• • •

I am full of energy and love. I extend this love to those in need. I don't need a reason to help others. A desire to give my time, money or energy is present within me and I help those who need me. I release my need to look good and give from an honest place. I don't need any reason to help, other than it makes me feel good.

• • •

What organization do I feel strongly about and how can I help?

I LOVE MY BODY BECAUSE OF WHAT IT HAS OVERCOME.

You may resist or reject a current body part or your entire body. Your body is a vehicle for love and it is always giving you guidance. Trust your body as it has overcome great changes. Learning to love yourself includes embracing your body as it is today. Love your flaws away and you will be free of self-inflected pain.

• • •

My body is a tool for transformation as it always guides me to the right path. I listen to my body and the wisdom within. I love every inch of my body and celebrate its strength and power. I am strong and beautiful and I love me.

• • •

Can I send love to every cell of my body? I
fill my body with light and love.

I AM COMPASSIONATE WITH MYSELF. IT TAKES TIME TO HEAL.

You are much too hard on yourself. Maybe you have recently experienced a loss of some kind. Others may tell you that you need to move on or get over the situation, but your true self knows it takes time to heal. Be compassionate with yourself during any time of grieving. All things take time. Allow the healing to happen of its' own accord.

• • •

I allow myself to heal. I give myself as much time as I need to move on from my past. I know my past has helped make me who I am today and I celebrate each moment that led to right now. I am kind to myself and give myself time to heal these open wounds. It is okay to be in the healing process. I will give it time.

• • •

Where have I been forcing myself to heal
faster than what feels right?

I STOP BLOWING MYSELF OFF.

Your needs are important. You may give most of your time and energy to others that you feel exhausted at the end of the day. Your desires matter and this is a reminder to make yourself a priority. When you show up for yourself, others will be more fulfilled too. You will find more balance when you stop blowing yourself off.

• • •

I show up for myself. My needs are important and it is necessary to listen to them in order to live a balanced life. When I put my needs first, I am showing self-respect and self-love to the world and myself. When I show up for me, I can be more valuable to others.

• • •

What loving act can I do for myself?

I DO NOT CHEAT ON MY FUTURE WITH MY PAST.

Have you been hanging out emotionally in your past? Perhaps your thoughts have been consumed with how a situation played out and you feel as though you have made a mistake. Maybe you can't forgive someone from your past and you spend your energy trying to fix the situation. The longer you stay in the past, the harder it is to move into your future. Forgive your past and you will welcome new opportunities into your life.

• • •

I am present in my life. I forgive my past so I can walk into my future. My future is waiting for me with open arms and enthusiasm. I welcome the new phase of my life and release my energetic hold on the past.

• • •

How have I been cheating on my future by
thinking thoughts of my past?

MY UNIQUENESS IS WHAT MAKES ME OUTSTANDING.

You are too down on yourself. Those flaws you hide are part of what makes you beautiful. You may be trying hard to fit in, but this is making you feel more like an outsider. You were not born to fit in. You are here to stand out. Stop giving so much attention to the things you find flawed or ugly and shine light on to the awesome you that is.

• • •

I am a unique child of the universe. All that I am I celebrate. My unique quirks are part of my beautiful being and I release my need to change myself to try to fit in. I am perfect as I am. I like me.

• • •

What "flaw" can I accept today?

I FLOOD MY FEAR BASED THOUGHTS WITH LOVE.

If there is an area of your life where you feel down and out, consider adding more love into the equation. You may be trying too hard to fight the situation, which makes you force a fake smile and pretend you are happy.

If you are trying to be happy, what you seek will elude you. Instead of looking to happiness as your answer, look to adding more love into the areas that feel fear-based. This can transform your life.

• • •

I let love in to all situations in my life. The more love I allow in, the happier I feel. It is safe to show the real me, which means I honor my needs in every moment. I show my feelings and this allows me to be happy in each moment. When I express myself, I honor myself.

• • •

Where can I invite more love in?

I AM ACCOUNTABLE
FOR MY OWN LIFE.

You may be blaming other people for your circumstances or situations. Instead of pointing the finger at others, turn it around to yourself. What role did you play in this situation? Now is the time to be responsible. This is not about self-inflected blame or punishing yourself. It is about taking responsibility so you can move forward.

Consider everything in your life (whether or not you like it) is made by design, by you. You get to choose what stays and goes. So if you are unhappy with an area of your life, you have the power to change it.

• • •

I am responsible for everything in my current reality. This is empowering because I can choose to remove anything and everything that no longer works for me. I do not blame myself for anything, nor do I punish others. Instead I take responsibility so I can move forward with clarity and focus.

• • •

What situation can I take responsibility for?

I BELIEVE THE WORLD IS ON MY SIDE AND I WILL SUCCEED.

You may feel closed down or shut out by a previous situation. Perhaps you shared a dream with another person and they told you it wasn't worth it. It is important to realize your dreams are part of your life plan. When you take a step forward, you are proving it can be done and you are worth it. Believe in yourself and you will be successful.

• • •

I am aligned with my dreams. I believe in my future self and the plan unfolding. I will succeed and show everyone how amazing I am. My dreams are important and I have great support around me. When I look for the good, I see the good. The world is on my side and ready to support me in my creative endeavors.

• • •

What dream do I want to prove can be done?

I AM NOT WHAT PEOPLE SAY I AM.

You might focus too much on what other people think of you. When others make comments or share their opinions, this has nothing to do with you. Learning to love yourself starts with releasing the need for approval from others. Focus all your attention on accepting yourself and you will be free of this external burden. Happiness can never come to you from the outside.

• • •

I am okay with where I am today. I am no longer disillusioned by others beliefs or opinions about me. The only thing I focus on is approving of my own self. I align with my truth, which is love and light. I matter and I know I make a difference.

• • •

Where have I been worrying too much about what others think?

I LEARN THE WAY ON THE WAY.

You may not feel ready to move forward on your planned path, but you are more ready than you realize. Now is the time to take action and move forward. The more self-confident you are, the more successful you will be. If you are unsure, that is okay. It is still necessary to take steps forward as your path will reveal itself one step at a time.

• • •

There are many doors open to me at this time. I graciously walk through them as I embrace new opportunities. I accept my path and grow through all challenges with a determination to succeed. The universe is supporting me and I will soar. My path becomes clear as I take more steps forward. I am confident and sure of myself.

• • •

Where have I been hesitating to take action?

I LET GO OF WHAT THE UNIVERSE IS ASKING ME TO RELEASE.

What are you holding onto? The universe has been guiding you to let go of certain things, habits or people in your life that no longer serve you. When you hold onto things past their expiration date, you are not being true to yourself. Go inward and listen to your heart. It will gently guide you into the next right action for releasing old ways of being.

• • •

I am open to living my life in expansive ways. I do this by releasing all old patterns, situation and people that no longer serve me. It is not mean or selfish to put myself first. It is an act of self-love. I see evidence of my love-filled actions when the universe guides me to new awareness and direction.

• • •

What has the universe been asking me to release?

I DON'T ROMANTICIZE THE PAST. I CHOOSE TO BE PRESENT.

You may be spending too much time focusing on the good aspects of the past. Although it is wonderful to see the positive sides of all situations, this could be clouding your judgment and view. When it comes to people or situations, there is what happens and what we perceived happened.

If you are only focusing on the good and failing to see the reality of the situation, you could set yourself up for failure in the future. Take off your rose-colored glasses and see the situation for what it really is.

• • •

I am connected to my true self in this moment. When I reflect back on previous situations, I can see all realities. Others motives are revealed to me when I take a nonreactive approach to my life. I step out of my past and choose to be present.

• • •

What past situation have I been romanticizing?
How has this hurt my ability to move forward?

MY ACTIONS ALIGN WITH MY WORDS.

Do your actions speak louder than your words? Do you do what you say you will do? Now is a good time to reflect and see if you can be more in tune with your true desires. If you say you want to do something, make sure your actions align to do it.

• • •

I am intentional with all of my interactions. I keep promises to others and myself. My words are graced with integrity and I am honest in all areas of my life.

• • •

In what ways have I been dishonest with myself by not following through on what I said I would do?

MY PLAN B COULD BE BETTER THAN PLAN A.

Are you holding onto a situation that no longer works? Perhaps you have recently gone through a change or transition and you are struggling to see the relevance. Sometimes the universe will push us into a new plan that contradicts our original path. Trust the universe is leading you to your true path and seek out guidance.

• • •

I am connected to my life's ultimate plan. I trust the universe and see the plan unfolding in front of me. I embrace new opportunities for growth and I expand with love and light.

• • •

What plan feels forced or like it no longer
fits in my life? Can I let it go?

I AM ENCHANTED WITH LIFE. I SEE THE BEAUTY IN EVERYTHING.

Life is opening up all around you. Learning to see the beauty in the seemingly small situations will open up your heart and mind. Look deep into your life and look at beauty in everything. Even washing the dishes can be an act of enchantment as you smell the bubbles and feel the warm water against your skin. In each activity you do, can you be more present?

• • •

I am enchanted with my life. I am in joy and see the good in every situation. I feel open and expansive as I embrace all of the world's beautiful creations.

• • •

Where can I pause and let more life in?

I AM NOT AFRAID TO ASK FOR HELP AND SUPPORT.

You may be taking on too much and trying to do it all yourself. If you are trying to be strong and assert your independent, now is the time to drop your guard. Asking for help is not a weakness. It is an act of self-love.

• • •

I am not afraid of my vulnerabilities. I actively seek out support from loved ones and accept their offer to support me. I am open to receiving love and I let this love in. It is safe to need help, for everyone needs one another.

• • •

What do I need support and who can I ask for help?

WHERE I LIVE FEELS LIKE A HOME.

Do you love where you live? Your home is your sanctuary and source of inspiration. If you live in an environment that strains your energy, consider adding more love. Now could be a good time to begin making arrangements to move into a place you like more. If it is not time for you to move, you can add more comfort into your home with candles, soft music and things you love.

• • •

My home is a reflection of my best self. I honor where I live and care for my place. I know my home is a sanctuary, which allows me to be my best self.

• • •

What does my home say about me?

HOW I FEEL IS MORE IMPORTANT THAN HOW I LOOK.

You might be worrying to much about what others think of you. If you are feeling self-doubt, self-loathing or self-blame, you might be trying to fit into the outside world. When you return to your true self, you will be reminded the only thing that really matters is how you feel. Focus more on how your life feels versus how it looks.

• • •

I feel good. I am connected to my best self and I choose healthy actions. I focus on how my life feels instead of how it looks. Happiness comes through my feelings and attention to the details of my life.

• • •

Where have I been more focused on how
I look rather than how I feel?

MY EMOTIONAL PAIN SHOWS ME WHAT NEEDS TO CHANGE.

Sadness, depression and heartache are gentle reminders to probe deeper into your life. Look at what is not working and be open to living your life in new ways. You will see that one day, it will all make sense.

• • •

I am connected to my emotions and I feel them fully. Any area of my life that feels painful is an opportunity for me to go inward. I reflect on my pain and see what needs to be changed.

• • •

Where in my life is the most pain and what is it trying to tell me?

NO ONE CAN MAKE ME FEEL "LESS THAN" WITHOUT MY PERMISSION.

You are worthy of your desires, but you have to believe in yourself first. If you are waiting for others to approve of you before you step forward, you may be doing yourself a disservice. Instead of giving your power away to others, align with your intentions and you will feel worthy of your desires.

• • •

I am worthy of my desires and connected to my best self. I let go of others' opinions, as they have no bearing on my overall choices in life. I feel powerful and aligned with my true self.

• • •

Where have I been feeling unworthy?

I APPRECIATE WHO I SEE IN THE MIRROR.

You are too hard on yourself, especially with your physical appearance. The person you see in the mirror is not someone to turn away from in disgust. That person you see is your best friend. That person knows your heart and your desires better than anyone else, so trust the person you see in the mirror. When you become friends with yourself, everything else falls into place.

• • •

I am my own best friend. I love everything about me and I appreciate who I see in the mirror. I matter in this world and my physical appearance is part of my life plan. The things I used to resist about me have become my greatest understanding for accessing my true self.

• • •

I will go to the mirror, look into my own eyes
and repeat "I love you" five times.

I AM PROUD TO BE VULNERABLE.

Showing your soft side is a beautiful experience. You don't need to hide your real emotions from those you love. When you go inward and trust yourself, you will see how important your emotions are. Showing the real you takes courage, and that is real vulnerability.

• • •

I am soft and approachable. I show others who I am by being honest with myself in each moment. When I am vulnerable, I am courageous. It is an act of love when I show my pride in who I am.

• • •

Who can I share my emotions with?

I CONSCIOUSLY CHOOSE MORE POSITIVE THOUGHTS.

Thinking positive thoughts is not naïve. It will help you see the big picture in everything. When you focus on the good in each situation, you open yourself up to receiving guidance on how to get through them. Choose positive thoughts to help you through all limiting situations.

• • •

I am deliberate with my thoughts. I choose uplifting thoughts that bring me joy. I see the good in all situations and I turn my attention to the positive aspects of everything.

• • •

What negative thoughts have I been carrying around?
How can I flip them into a positive?

I HAVE DETERMINATION AND WILL POWER.

You may feel shattered by recent setbacks. But getting back on the horse is part of your overall plan. Persistence is important right now as you reach your goal. Today is confirmation you have what it takes to reach your potential. Take steps out of your comfort zone and try new routines. The bravery you show will reward you with confidence and joy.

• • •

I am connected to my higher self. I am proud of how far I have come and see all my setbacks as miracles in disguise. I am determined and will reach my goals with effortless grace and ease. I am empowered and connected to my accomplishments. I take pride in how far I've come.

• • •

Where can I allow myself to feel more pride
in what I have accomplished?

I HAVE A SUPPORT SYSTEM THAT WOULD DO ANYTHING FOR ME.

You are not alone. You have amazing people around you who you can gain strength and courage from. Others are available to help you when you allow the support into your life. The meaning you are seeking will come through interactions with others and the support you receive.

• • •

I am open to other people's guidance and support. The challenges in my life will be removed when I seek out help. I am being guided to the right mentors, friends and relationships to assist me for my highest good.

• • •

How can I get out of my comfort zone and
ask a new friend for support?

NEW CHOICES BRING NEW RESULTS.

You may feel stuck or as though your life is in a static mode. If you have been working hard to try to achieve specific goals or solve troubling situations, you may be ready to give up. Today is a reminder to keep going, but consider a new approach to solving old problems. When you step out of your comfort zone and try new things, you will see refreshing results.

• • •

I am open to trying new things. I solve old problems in fresh, innovate ways. I connect with my true self to align with my greatest good. When I move forward with confidence, I am at ease.

• • •

What can I try again but in a new way?

I EMBRACE MY EMOTIONS.

Your emotions are trying to tell you something. Listen to the wisdom within. When you feel sad, let yourself feel the emotions. It is okay to cry and be vulnerable. If you are happy, allow yourself to feel the happiness. You might be pushing your emotions aside in an effort to maintain status quo. When you embrace your emotions, you will be free.

• • •

I am fully present with my emotions. I allow myself to feel each feeling as it arises. When I feel my emotions, they help guide me to a deeper awareness of self-actualization. My emotions are a strong guidance system. I trust them.

• • •

What emotion have I been hiding? I allow myself to feel them.

I CELEBRATE OTHERS SUCCESSES.

Do you feel jealous or concerned that others have something you want? When you focus your attention on the lack of what you want, you keep yourself from receiving. Instead of condemning others for their success and opportunities, celebrate them as if they were your own. The universe is abundant and full of opportunity for all. You will get what you desire when you hold love and light for others.

• • •

I am alive and full of life. I set myself up for success by celebrating all good things in life. When others are rewarded, I sing in the praise of joy alongside them. I am connected to my life and I celebrate others wins as if they are my own. There is no place for jealousy in my life. I turn all my attention to what I want and use others success as a possibility for my own future.

• • •

Whose recent success can I celebrate, and congratulate them on a job well done?

I IMAGINE MYSELF LIVING MY IDEAL LIFE.

A part of you might not believe in the power of your dreams. Moving forward, it is important for you to focus on what you want and spend time visualizing your success. Your imagination is your most powerful asset in reaching your dream life. When you can believe it *before* you actually see it, you will be successful in creating your future. Trust the visions that come to you and imagine yourself living the life you truly want.

• • •

My goals have already manifested and I am living my ideal life. I spend time everyday imagining myself in my ideal life and this helps create my plan forward. Each action step I take gives me more clarity on how to reach my dream life. I am living my ideal life in each moment.

• • •

What does my ideal life look and feel like?

I IMAGINE MYSELF
LIVING MY IDEAL LIFE.

I NURTURE MY INSTINCTS.

You have an internal guidance system guiding you in every moment of your life. Your instincts are your strongest force forward. Nurture them with love and give your gut feelings more priority in your life. Your instincts will never lead you astray.

• • •

I listen to the internal voice that guides me forward. I have an awareness of self that allows me to confidently move forward in life with conviction and attention to detail. I nurture my instincts by trusting myself in each new situation.

• • •

What are my instincts trying to tell me about
a situation that has caused me angst?

MY CREATIVE PURSUITS ARE REWARDED.

Your ideas matter and pursuing your creative side is important right now. You may feel uncreative or uninspired, but honoring your creative impulses will serve you well. Being creative is not about what you do or how it looks. It is about what you experience. Give yourself permission to be more creative and express your artistic side. You will be rewarded for expressing your free-flowing nature.

• • •

I am open to showing my creative side. I have ideas worthy of pursuing. When I am inspired, I act and my creative pursuits are always rewarded. When I am creative and honor my expressive nature, I am free and open to inspiration.

• • •

What creative project can I start?

I AM A LEADER TO THOSE AROUND ME.

You may enjoy the subtle role of following others, but today is an opportunity for you to honor the leader inside you. You have unique gifts and a story that can resonate with others. Everything you have been through and all of your life experience can benefit others. Just by showing up for yourself and honoring your true needs, you become a leader to those around you. Trust yourself as you step into the leadership role of your life.

• • •

I inspire others just by being true to myself. My past has prepared me to stand tall and align with my truth. I am confidant and connected to myself, and when I show up for myself, I show up for the world. I am a leader when I am true to myself, as this is reflected onto others.

• • •

What area of my life can I take more of a leadership role in?

I AM UNAPOLOGETIC ABOUT WHAT MAKES ME HAPPY.

You might be putting too much emphasis on other people opinions of you and your actions. Return to your desires and get in touch with why you want them. When you connect with the why, this will move you forward with energetic ease. The more you do that makes you happy, the happier you will be. It won't matter what others think about you or your life because you will be living your authentic joy.

• • •

I am connected to my joy. I do what makes me happy and this in turn makes others happy. When I align with my honest desires, I am rewarded with love and support. I am unapologetic about who I am and what I love.

• • •

Where can I be more unapologetic about what brings me joy?

I AM MY OWN BEST FRIEND.

Turn to yourself for more guidance and insight. Treat yourself as you would your own best friend. Look at yourself with non-judgmental eyes and embrace yourself for your unique beauty. You wouldn't judge or talk down to a friend, so stop doing it to yourself. It is essential for you to befriend yourself and start to see the amazing person you really are.

• • •

I am kind to myself and I treat myself with respect. I turn to myself as I do a real friend. I have good insight and awareness and I trust me. I love every part of myself and I refrain from judgment and self-blame. I am connected to love and I shine love out into the world. My truth is love.

• • •

How can I create a better relationship with myself?

I'M NOT AFRAID TO THINK OUTSIDE THE BOX.

Exciting new opportunities are on their way to you. They will come much faster when you give yourself permission to step outside of the comfort zone. You might feel complacent or bored with situations in your life.

Maybe things are at a standstill and you feel like things aren't working out as you want. The situation can transform when you think from a new perspective. Consider you have been focusing on the problem with tunnel vision. To rejuvenate your life, think outside the box and be more playful with your approach.

• • •

I am in harmony with my life. Everything in my life fully comes together and I am in a state of flow. I am not afraid of trying new things and I am open to living my life in fresh new ways.

• • •

Where have I been playing it safe?

I AM COMFORTABLE IN THE SILENCE.

When was the last time you allowed yourself to sit in silence? Silence is an important balance to a happy life. Allow silence to guide your true focus forward. Instead of trying to control conversations or situations by filling them with words, consider a more quiet approach. Being in silence can open up new clarity for your life. You will have a remarkable awareness of your true self when you allow silence to guide you forward.

• • •

I am comfortable in silence. I do not need to fill my quiet time with words and noise. Instead of panic or constriction, I release my fears and I let love in. Silence is an opening to guidance I want to receive. When I am silent, I can hear my heart speak. I honor silence.

• • •

Can I sit in silence for a few minutes a day?
(Give it a try now.)

I RETREAT INWARD FOR INSPIRATION.

You have motivation and strength inside of you. Turning inward will help inspire your life in all areas. Show more gentleness to yourself and see the connection to everything. Your inside world will reflect into your outer world. Any situation you find yourself in will require a more sensitive approach by retreating inward for ultimate inspiration.

• • •

What I am is love. What I choose to manifest is more love. My true self inspires everything I do, which is a reflection of true love. I am full of love and kindness and compassion, and I express my real self to the world. In all my experiences, I choose to focus inward for answers.

• • •

How can I allow more inspiration in my life?

I AM EMPOWERED AND IN CONTROL OF MY LIFE.

Recent situations may have caused you concern, but align with your true self and you will see you are never out of control. You may feel a lot of concerns around your life. You can make a choice to harmonize yourself with love. You no longer have to worry or live out your fear. Instead, turn your attention to the perfections you already have.

• • •

I am in control of my life. I am empowered because I align all my choices with love. I am a creator of my own life and I am willing to show more love to others and myself. I am the example for others of what is possible in life because I am in control of my life.

• • •

What situations can I celebrate in my life?

NOTHING IS FOREVER.

You may feel stuck or perhaps you are experiencing a recent loss. Embracing the notion that nothing lasts forever will help you see the impermanence of life as a gift. This is an empowering approach to life because it can help you be more present in every situation.

If you are struggling to accept a situation in your life, know this too shall pass. Nothing is forever, which can work in your favor. The body you dislike, the unsatisfying relationship or job will soon be out of your experience. Be confident in knowing the present is all you have and no two moments are the same.

• • •

I am in the present moment of my life. I release all of my old behaviors and insecurities so I can be present in this moment. I let go of all troubling perspectives and allow more love into my life. I know nothing is forever, which helps me shine more light onto the present.

• • •

Where can I be more present in my life?

WHAT I SEE IN LIFE DEPENDS GREATLY ON WHAT I'M LOOKING FOR.

What you see in your life is a reflection of your original focus. What you put your attention on will manifest. If you are dissatisfied with results in your life, return to your thought patterns about the situation. If you want more joy-filled results, focus on more positive thoughts.

• • •

I am aligned with my original intentions. All is in right order in my life because I am actively living the results of my actions and loving thoughts. I am connected to my truth. I am happy with the results in my life.

• • •

What results am I dissatisfied with and
how can I reframe my focus?

MY LIFE IS IN PERFECT BALANCE WHEN I LISTEN TO MY HEART.

The key to success in your life is balance. If you are feeling overwhelmed or stressed out, take a deep breath in and return inward to your heart. In order to create successful solutions, you need to align with what brings you joy in the moment. This is a balancing act you can master. When you make choices from a deliberate place of love, you are more calm and peaceful and your life is in balance.

• • •

I focus on my accomplishments, for I've done a great job. My life is in perfect balance because I take care of myself and follow my heart. I honor my needs. I allow myself to be recognized and I embrace the power of the pause. I take care of my needs and honor my inner desires. My life is in perfect balance when I listen to my heart.

• • •

What is my heart telling me?

I TAKE GREAT PRIDE IN ALL I DO.

You are doing excellent work but chances are you are not celebrating your successes. Trust that the efforts you have put into everything will pay off. When you hold the intention of abundance, rewards can come to you. Focus on your long-term goals and take pride in all you do.

• • •

I am proud of who I am. Everything I do is inspired by a loving place and I take inspired action forward. I have learned so much on my journey and all of my life lessons have been a benefit to my divine life's plan and me.

• • •

How can I show more pride in who I am?

WHEN I GIVE I ALSO RECEIVE.

Perhaps you have been holding on too tightly to your finances. When you share resources with others, more abundance can come to you. You may feel like you don't have enough time or money to share with others, but this may mean you are holding on too tightly. When resources are not shared, it will close off and block the abundant energy from coming to you. Also pay attention to your energy and emotions. Are you giving enough of yourself to the world?

• • •

I am happy to share my true self with others. I give my time and energy to those who are in need of support. My resources can help others and I share my gifts openly and without expectations. When I give, I receive so much more in return.

• • •

Where can I give more time, money or resources?

I MAKE A DIFFERENCE.

You might be going through a difficult life situation and you could be feeling vulnerable. If you continue to seek out validation from others, you may never feel the love you truly desire. When you love and approve of yourself first, everything else will fall into place. Start by knowing you matter and you are a gift to the world.

• • •

I matter and I make a difference in this world. When I connect to my heart, I can show my true self and shine forward. The world needs me as I am. I am perfect just as I am. I make a valuable contribution to the world and I confidently show my true self.

• • •

What difference do I make?

I GO BEFORE I KNOW.

You may feel unsure of which direction to go in your life. Perhaps you are at a crossroads or you are unclear which route to take. Today is a gentle reminder that unless you take a step forward, the path will not reveal itself. When you take action, even before you know the right path, you will instantly see the right direction for you. Trust yourself and go before you know.

• • •

I am confident even when I do not know the best move forward. I take action by aligning myself with my internal light. When I connect to my inspiration, I can move forward with conviction and clarity. I go before I know.

• • •

What action step can I take despite my insecurity or lack of confidence?

NEW OPPORTUNITIES FOR HAPPINESS ARE ON THEIR WAY TO ME.

You can throw your hands in the air and declare, "It's over." Perhaps a situation has recently ended in your life and now is time for celebration. You can look to your future and see opportunities coming your way. Happiness is a choice and it starts with you turning your focus to the happy times instead of the bad.

• • •

I see happiness all around me. I focus my energy on the good in my life, which removes the bad. I know new opportunities are part of my life's plan and I am open to receiving more happiness and love.

• • •

What happy times can I focus on?

I BREAK FREE FROM ALL THAT IS HOLDING ME BACK.

You are not your past, nor do you need to spend any more time focusing your energy on what has happened to you. Instead of spending time thinking about what could go wrong or what has gone wrong, see these as just fears from your past trying to replay in the present. You are bigger than anything that can ever happen to you, so turn inward and release the confines of fear. You are stronger than you will ever know.

• • •

I am strong, determined, focused and excited for my future. I refuse to let my past stop me from moving forward. I am a trailblazer, blazing a trail of happiness and hope wherever I go. I am free from my past. Nothing will ever stand in my way. All I desire is possible and on its way to me.

• • •

What is standing in my way and how can I release its hold on me?

I DON'T FEAR MY FUTURE. I KNOW IT WILL WORK OUT.

Everything happens for a reason. Perhaps you are focusing on a recent loss or major life change. When you connect with your heart, you will see positive things are on their way to you.

Although things may not have turned out as you planned, the universe is looking out for you and this transition is nothing to fear. It will all work out in your favor. Believe in your future and trust things are working out for the best.

• • •

I know things are always in right order. Everything happens for a reason and I believe in the power of good. Even though I can't see how things could work out, I trust the process and I know I am being guided. I embrace the unknown and welcome my future.

• • •

Where can I put more faith in the process?

THE FASTEST WAY TO IMPROVE MY SELF-CONFIDENCE IS TO DO THE THING I FEAR.

You may feel insecure and shy. But today is a reminder that the very thing you fear is what will bring you freedom. When you move through your fear and take loving action forward, your insecurities will fade. Confidence comes through taking action steps, your fear will disappear and be replaced with love when you take action steps forward.

• • •

I am fearless and free of worry. My self-confidence is flourishing as I step into my future with love and purpose. My fear is only an indication of what I care about and I bust through all fears with action steps forward.

• • •

How can I bust through my fear?

I ACCEPT EVERYTHING I AM — AND AM NOT.

Your own self-approval is essential for a happy life. Stop trying to get everyone else to approve of you and instead spend loving energy on cultivating your own worth. You are beautiful and perfect as you are. Embrace everything you stand for and celebrate all that is you.

• • •

I accept who I am and release my need to change myself. I no longer need the approval of others as I love and approve of myself. My light shines forward with love and compassion.

• • •

What insecurity can I love today?

I AM ONLY TRAPPED BY MY ILLUSION.

You might be experiencing a situation that feels constricting or forced upon you. Today is a reminder you are only trapped by your current focus on the situation. From a spiritual standpoint, everything we experience is an illusion of separation from love. If you feel emotional pain or turmoil, you may be trapped in fear.

To break free from this, look at the illusion of what is versus what could be. Surround your "what could be" with love and you will glide through all troubling times.

• • •

I am not a victim of my current situation. I focus my thoughts on loving energy and choose to see the truth in all troubling situations. I know I am capable of moving through difficult times and I am only trapped by my negative thoughts. I turn to positive expectations and I am free.

• • •

What *could* be in my life? I spend time focusing on what
I want instead of what I don't want.

I FIND A WAY TO KEEP GOING.

Your motivation may be dwindling. Remind yourself why you started and keep focus on the big picture. You will benefit from making mini goals within your big plan. Setting smaller attainable goals will help you stay on track. If the situation you are losing motivation with feels forced, do not push it. You will be better off taking a more playful, relaxed approach than powering through it. Take a break, go for a walk, take a bath or treat yourself to a tasty treat. You will return to your situation with refreshed eyes and determination.

• • •

I am focused and free of fear of failure. I am worthy of my goals and they are coming true for me. My motivation comes from inspiration from my heart. I align with my truth, which keeps me on track. I add more child-like wonder to my projects and I feel happy and free.

• • •

What am I trying to power through? Can I
consider a more fun-loving approach?

I SEND MY ENEMIES LOVE AND LIGHT.

You might be spending too much time emotionally drained because you are in anger. If you know someone who has harmed you or caused you pain, rise above the situation with love. You can take the high road and choose to disengage from the situation. You do this with forgiveness and by sending them love and light.

• • •

I release all worry and pain caused by others. I forgive them, for they know not what they do. When people hurt my feelings, I retract my anger by focusing on surrounding myself with love and light. I wish others no harm. I wish those who have offended me compassion and love. We are all connected and when I send love to those who need it most, I heal myself too.

• • •

What enemy can I send love?

IT IS REFRESHING TO GIVE LIFE TO OLD PROJECTS.

You have really good ideas. You should give yourself more credit for the projects you started in the past. Instead of feeling like a failure, look at the projects as opportunities for growth. Through each venture, you have learned more about what you want and don't want out of your life. Perhaps there is one project you want to return to. Get back into the joy of the process of creating and enjoy the journey.

• • •

I am full of creative energy and lighthearted fun. My inspiration flows. I return to old projects with new life. It is refreshing to revisit old projects as they help me explore my creative side. My ideas are powerful and they want to manifest into full form.

• • •

What project can I give new life to?

IT ISN'T WHO I AM THAT HOLDS ME BACK. IT'S WHO I THINK I AM NOT.

You might spend too much time focusing on what you can't do. Instead of spreading the negative energy, focus your thoughts on what you are capable of. You have a life force inside you far greater than you could ever imagine. Put your attention on your talents, strengths and good qualities. This will help you feel more secure and confident.

• • •

I have talents and strengths unique to my life purpose. I celebrate my strengths and show them openly with love. When I connect to my heart, I am guided by my intuition and I am connected to my real self. I focus on who I am rather than allowing my fears to dictate who I am not.

• • •

What part of myself is holding onto fear? How can I let it go?

THINGS MOVE FAST WHEN THEY ARE RIGHT.

When things are in right order, they move at an effortless pace forward. If there is an area of your life that feels strained or forced, this is a reminder to stop pushing. You will find freedom in the flow. When you are on the right path, things will flow fast and with great momentum. Enjoy the ride and trust you are being led into the right direction for your big picture.

• • •

I am in a constant state of flow. My life unfolds effortlessly and I am along for the ride. There is nothing I have to force, for all my plans are falling naturally into place. When things are aligned with my highest good, they happen rapidly. I am being divinely guided and I trust this inspiration that comes to me. I take motivated action forward. My life is unfolding in right order.

• • •

What situation in my life has great momentum and forward movement?

I SEE THE TRUTH IN ALL SITUATIONS.

When you seek the truth in all situations, you will feel liberated. It is essential for you to be honest with yourself. Stop candy-coating situations or trying to hide behind excuses. If you are settling in a relationship or with specific habits in your own life, this is a reminder to seek out the truth of the matter. Focus on your true desires and what you deserve. We accept the love we think we deserve, so look inward to regain confidence in your worth.

• • •

I am honest with myself about my values and approach to life. I release all relationships and habits that hinder my ability to be happy. When I return to my heart, I seek the answers I need.

• • •

Where have I been dishonest with myself?

THERE IS LIGHT AT THE END OF THE TUNNEL.

The situation you are in has already come to an end. From a big picture sense, your life is unfolding according to plan. When you retreat inward, you can see the purpose in your pain. Every situation you have experienced has groomed you for the next chapter of your life. Instead of dwelling on the sadness, focus on the silver lining and the light at the end of the tunnel.

• • •

I am okay. My life may not be perfect but it is perfect in this moment. I allow myself to feel every part of my journey, which means I am present and aware. I see the light inside of me as it reflects out into the world. When I follow the light, the darkness disappears.

• • •

What is the silver lining of my current situation?

I AM IN A STATE OF FLOW.

When you do what you love, you are in a joyful state. Tapping into joy is possible when you follow your heart and do what you love. If you are at a standstill in an area of your life, then focus on bringing in more joy. Find value in the process and you will feel inner peace.

• • •

I am in the moment and I allow my life to unfold naturally. I am in a state of flow, which means I trust the universe is co-creating with me to help support my life's plan. There is nothing for me to do or fix. I release all worry, for everything is always taken care of. I am abundant and successful. I am in a state of flow.

• • •

Where can I relax and stop trying to control the situation?

I KNOW WHEN TO MOVE ON.

You don't need to stay in any situation that has expired. You might be holding onto a relationship that is supposed to end. Sometimes when we grow onto a personal development path, our friends or loved ones don't always come along. If you have someone in your life bringing you down, consider this a sign it is time to move on.

• • •

I know when to move on. I don't hold onto anything that is supposed to be set free. I listen to my inner voice, which tells me when it is time to seek out new friendships and release the old. I energetically cut the tie between negative friends and family. I connect to my own love and light.

• • •

What relationship can I remove myself from?

THERE ARE INFINITE RESOURCES AVAILABLE FOR ME.

You might feel lack or focus on your limitations. Instead of spending your energy looking at what is not with you, turn your attention to what you do have. You have multiple solutions available. You just have to be willing to see new opportunities. There are infinite resources available to you. Trust you will be guided to the right one for you.

• • •

I am guided to release all limitations and negative beliefs. I turn my attention inward to seek my truth. I align with my heart's desires, which will show me the next best right action. I step lovingly into my future with open arms as I embrace all the resources available to me. I am only limited by my thoughts. I release all limitations with love.

• • •

What resources can I use to help me solve a troubling problem?

MY ANXIETY IS NOT BASED ON REALITY.

The entrapment you feel is not real. It is inspired by fear. The anxiety in your life is often based on false beliefs and fear-based thoughts. Turn your fears over to the universe and trust you will receive the peace you desire. What you crave is inner peace and you will get that as you continue to show up for yourself and seek out guidance through mentors, new friendships and connections with yourself.

• • •

My anxiety is not real. It is inspired by fear and I release my limitations to the universe. The clarity I seek comes from my connection with self. The more I am in tune with my body and heart, the easier my life will be. I let go of my worry and replace it with love.

• • •

What anxiety can I release?

I AM TENACIOUS WITH MY GOALS. THEY ARE ACTUALIZED WITH LOVE.

Focus on your dreams with energy and passion. When you put love into the equation, your dreams manifest faster. Be tenacious and unapologetic about your desires. Your goals are part of your life plan. When you follow through on the inspiration that comes to your heart, you are living your purpose.

• • •

I am in love with my life and my dreams are coming true. I shine light on all areas of my life so I can remove the shadows and negative thoughts that once limited me. When I focus on my goals with passion and love, I will not fail. The universe is supporting me in my life plan, as my ultimate wishes come true every day.

• • •

What goal can I add more love to?

I PROMOTE MYSELF
WITH CONFIDENCE.

You might be feeling insecure about showing your true self. Whether you are preparing yourself for a first date, asking your boss for a raise or starting your own business, owning your worth is the key to success. Promote yourself with a radiant light and allow the real you to shine through. When you are comfortable with yourself, your confidence is infectious.

• • •

I get what I want by being true to myself. I am confident and aligned with my heart. When I show my true self, people respect and admire me. I shine my inner light onto others and promote my true self with grace and ease.

• • •

What insecure am I ready to release?

I AM WELL.

The wellness you seek is already inside of you. You may be feeling rundown or focused on disease. When you focus your attention on the disharmony in your body, you bring more attention to what is not working. Instead, focus on sending love and light to every one of your cells and picture your body healed.

• • •

I am well. I am harmony and I am light. I send loving energy to every cell in my body. I replace all disharmony with comfort and ease. I send love to my areas of pain and focus on healing and resolution. My body is a tool of greater understanding to my true self. I am at ease with my body and my life."

• • •

What thoughts of disharmony can I heal with loving thoughts?

I AM CALM IN THE CHAOS.

Situations may be around you that you cannot control. Perhaps it feels like the walls are caving in. You may not be able to control those around you, but you can always control your own internal state. When you align with your own heart center, nothing will affect your true balance.

• • •

I align to my heart's center and seek out the truth in all situations. What once bothered me no longer affects me, for I am peace and harmony. I can be calm in the chaos because I am a beacon of love and light.

• • •

Where can I release my need to control my environment and allow things to be?

I REPLACE JUDGMENT WITH CURISOTY?

You may be trying to solve a problem by thinking your way through it. Perhaps your motivation has eluded you and the project has come to a standstill. Instead of forcing analytic thoughts into the equation, reflect your attention out into the world. Go explore life and watch your productivity increase.

• • •

I am connected to all of life and see it as a balance and flow. I am inspired by my own experience and the life force energy around me. Everything I experience and everyone I meet is an opportunity to learn more about life and myself. I replace all judgment with curiosity.

• • •

What inspires me?

EVERY DAY I ASK MYSELF,
"DID I MAKE A DIFFERENCE?"

EVERY DAY I ASK MYSELF, "DID I MAKE A DIFFERENCE?"

You may feel as though you are not doing enough to help others. You have a desire inside of you to make a difference and connect with other people. Know you are living your true purpose when you are helping others and you do this every day.

Just by being you, and being true to your heart, you have the power to help others. It is not how many people you help that matters. It is the fact that you helped. Focus on what you can give instead of what you can get.

• • •

Instead of judging myself or putting pressure on myself, I align with my true intentions of love and respect. I am connected to my true self and I align with my heart's desire, which is supporting and helping others. I ask myself, "Did I make a difference?" And I know each day I do.

• • •

What difference did I make today?

I KNOW IT IS NOT ABOUT ME.

You might be over-analyzing and over-thinking a situation. When events unfold and other people are involved, it is easy to fall into victim mode and wonder why they did or didn't do what you thought they would. Today's focus is on the inner knowing that you don't have to take things personally.

What others do is a reflection of their own beliefs, fears and thought patterns. Not everything is about you. Detach yourself from the attachment to others. Also now is a good time to look at where you have been selfish in your life. Consider it isn't always about you. Reaching out to apologize to someone might be helpful for you to move on.

• • •

I disengage with the drama around me and I know what others do is not about me. I also look at my life and look at where I can add more love and self-compassion. I may have unknowingly hurt another person. It is my intention to make things right.

• • •

Who can you apologize too?

I PASSED THE TEST.

You did it. It's time for celebration. You have recently experienced a challenging event or situation and you overcame the challenge. Life is full of lessons and opportunities for growth. You will continue to repeat patterns until you learn the lessons. If there is a situation you recently found yourself in, where you acted with new awareness, you have arrived at a new level of understanding. You passed the test and can celebrate your victory.

• • •

I am the creator of my life and I show up fully. I dive into each situation with awareness, compassion and honesty. I remove unnecessary patterns in my life by being present and asking what I can learn.

• • •

What patterns keep repeating in my life and what can I learn from them?

I DETACH FROM THE DRAMA AROUND ME.

Situations, drama and life events will always be unfolding around you. You have a choice to play into the drama or remove yourself from it. Your life will be productive and you will feel more peace when you detach from the drama. You dreams will manifest faster and you will feel the peace you seek.

• • •

I remove myself from unnecessary drama and chaos. Everything I need is inside of me and I focus inward for survival. The less I allow the outside world in, the safer, more secure and peaceful I am.

• • •

What drama can I disengage with?

I EXPLORE ALL MY OPTIONS.

You need not tunnel vision your way through any situation. Perhaps you have been to narrow-minded in your approach. Maybe you feel trapped and can see no way out. Take a step back and look at all angles of the situation.

You have multiple resources available to you and many ways to solve this particular dilemma. Instead of focusing on the path that causes the most resistance, expand your search beyond. Be open to receiving guidance and support.

• • •

I am open to receiving guidance and support. I explore multiple angles and options as there are infinite solutions available me. I trust everything is working out in my favor and I move forward with effortless confidence and trust.

• • •

Where have I been too narrow-minded?

I'VE DONE NOTHING WRONG.

You put too much blame on yourself. You have done nothing wrong, yet you feel like it is your fault. The situations in your life are all part of a greater understanding to your greater good. Instead of thinking things didn't work out, start celebrating things always fall into place.

When you can shift your focus on what is wonderful instead of the lack, you will feel more connected to your true self. Forgive yourself and know you did the best you could with what you knew at the time.

• • •

I forgive myself for all my past mistakes. I see now that nothing was out of order and wrong. My mistakes are actually an opportunity for deeper awareness within myself. I cultivate self-love and inner peace through my situations and retreat inward for guidance. I know I have not done anything wrong. It is not my fault. I release self-blame and focus on love. I invite light in.

• • •

What can I forgive myself for?

I AM ALIGNED WITH
MY INTENTION.

Stop focusing on what you don't want and return to why you started. When you recalibrate and refocus your attention back onto your desires, you remove fear and emotional distress. If you have been focusing on what could go wrong, shift your attention to what could go right. And align inward to your inner heart, which is love.

• • •

Everything I desire is connected to my heart center. I choose to bring more love into my life by following my heart with intention and focus. I connect to my passion, which leads me to my purpose. I am always aligned with my highest good and I trust everything is always in right order.

• • •

What is my intention?

I DON'T DO ANYTHING I DON'T WANT TO DO.

If you feel pressure to do anything, stop and return to the present moment. Anxieties can take over and prevent you from seeing the situation clearly. Whether the pressure comes from demands of the outside world, an internal deadline or pressure you've placed upon yourself, ask yourself, "Is this really what I want?" When you listen to the answer, you will be guided forward with love.

• • •

I only do what I want to do, when I want to do it. I do all things with great love. When I make progress in my life, it is because I am connected to my joy and what feels right. I release all pressure timed to deadlines and external demands. Instead, I turn to light, love, my inspiration and my truth.

• • •

What do I feel forced to do and how can I
bring more joy into the situation?

I DON'T SECOND-GUESS MYSELF.

Stop second-guessing yourself. Everything you've ever gone through has prepared you for this. You can do it. Believe in yourself. The only thing stopping you is fear, based on insecurity and worry. But you are more ready than you give yourself credit for.

• • •

I am ready for this. I can do this and I am confident in my skills and talents. I know that the ideas that come to me are part of my life's plan, so I act with courage and grace as I move forward.

• • •

What am I worried about?
How can I move forward and stop second-guessing myself?

I TAKE TIME TO REST.

Your body needs time to heal. You have been working extremely hard and pushing to make new things fall into place. Instead of working so hard, retreat inward and seek the celebration in the pause. Taking time to rest will help cultivate a deeper awareness of productivity and focus. You may feel like you are missing out and that is why you are working so hard. But when you can slow down and relax, you give what you want a chance to come to you.

If you feel unproductive and cannot relax, use today to experience relaxation. Can you go for a nature walk, sit in silence and let meditation become a practice? Will you take a nice bath or read a new book? Taking time to rest is an act of self-love. When you rest, you show the universe you trust the divine order of everything.

• • •

I am productive and successful. All of my goals are being met because I balance my time well. I encourage relaxation and seek out ways to care for myself. I listen to my heart and let my body tell me what it needs. The wisdom in my body is the key to my success. I understand the power in the pause and return to the present moment when I relax.

• • •

How can I relax today?

I AM FLOODED WITH GRATITUDE.

There is infinite energy and support around you at all times. When you feel down and out, immediately turn your attention to the love and support around you and within your soul. When you look, you will see how abundant, successful, pretty and happy you already are. Look onto your life with gratitude and allow this energy to flood through all interactions. Being grateful will help cultivate more abundance and love in your life. Gratitude is the life force of everything.

• • •

I give thanks to all that is in my life. I do not focus on any negativity or drama, but instead hold space for opportunities and expansive growth. I know everything is working out for my greatest good. I trust divine timing and celebrate all the good in my life. I am grateful for everything.

• • •

What am I most thankful for today?

THE UNIVERSE REMOVES ALL OBSTACLES IN MY WAY.

Fear not for the barriers you currently face, are only temporary. You will overcome them by asking the universe for help. The universe is your best buddy in removing situations and barriers to your overall well-being. Instead of forcing your way through any tough situation, ask the universe for help and be open to receiving the guidance.

• • •

I trust the universe, my heart and higher power. I know my heart will help me stay focused and align with loving energy. The universe will remove all unnecessary obstacles from my life, including obstacles I no longer fear. I am coasting through the journey of life.

• • •

What barrier and fear can I ask the universe to help me remove?

I SEE LOVE EVERYWHERE.

Believe in miracles and the power of good. When you look for evidence of love, your will see it everywhere. Miracles are manifestations of love and support. Allow yourself to witness and be present for all that is great.

• • •

I believe in miracles. I see them everywhere I look. I know I am a miracle and when I shine my light, I help others. I trust the universe is working with me to release all worry and fear. I am being led with intention and loving energy. I am a miracle.

• • •

What miracle have I recently witnessed?

THERE IS NOTHING TO FIX.

You may be trying to change yourself to reach a new ideal or form of perfection. Perhaps you want to fix your crooked teeth, your body weight or your hair. Your body is a unique vehicle for love. Ask those you respect and care about if they notice the flaws you intended to fix. The answers may surprise you, as you are your own worst critic. The way you see yourself is not the way the rest of the world sees you. Turn your focus to more loving energy and accept yourself as you are. You are a beautiful child of the universe.

• • •

There is nothing wrong with me. My insecurities and flaws are actually unique quirks that make me special. Instead of fighting aspects of my body I don't like, I accept myself with grace and love. My outside body is not a reflection of my inner light. I choose to fix what will empower me, but from a loving, heartfelt place. I know the way I am today is perfect.

• • •

What aspect of myself can I send more love
to instead of critical thoughts?

EVERYTHING HAPPENS
FOR A REASON.

When you hold onto any area of your life that might not be working, you resist the natural flow. You may be concerned or worried about a situation that has not worked out to your liking. Now is a perfect opportunity to turn into your heart and seek comfort.

You future self knows all is in right order and everything in your life, even the seemingly uncomfortable setbacks, are part of divine plan. Instead of turning to worry, focus on how you feel throughout the situation. Align your energy with love and you will feel more at peace.

• • •

I trust the perfect timing to everything in my life. What may feel like a setback is actually a removal of what no longer served me in my life. I turn my focus to love and joyful thoughts as I connect to my true self. I know everything and everyone in my life is on purpose and I embrace each situation as if I choose it myself.

• • •

What area of my life feels like a setback but
might actually be a blessing in disguise?

I SEEK OUT SANCTUARY.

A lot of information is coming at you at every moment of the day. It is wise for you to seek out time to retreat inward and find sanctuary. Take time each week to show up for yourself by removing yourself from technological distractions and current events. Treat yourself to life's simple luxuries and feel your soul uplift in joy.

• • •

I allow my soul to rejuvenate by treating it to the simple pleasures of life. I rest in the moment and seek out sanctuary for my sprit. When I unplug and pause, I rediscover a new sense of self, one full of peace and joy.

• • •

What sanctuary can I seek?

I DON'T LIE.

Where are you denying yourself your true desires? Get honest with yourself and look at any lies you are telling yourself about your life. Perhaps "Things aren't really as bad as they seem," "I don't deserve to happy," "God is punishing me," "I will never be happy." Look closely at the limiting thoughts you tell yourself.

You may pride yourself on being honest with others, but if you lie to yourself you are hurting everyone. Send yourself love and kindness and look at each lie with a willing to shift awareness.

• • •

I am honest and in integrity with myself. I keep my promises and tell myself the truth. If anything in my life is not working, I am honest about the situation and I let go of the attachment. I care for myself with love and appreciation. I honor my life by being honest with me.

• • •

What lies am I telling myself?
How can I be more honest?

I ALLOW THINGS TO BE WHAT THEY ARE IN THEIR OWN TIME AND PLACE.

There is nothing you have to do or anyone you need to change. You may be frustrated with someone else's actions or behaviors, but this is a reminder that the power of peace is within you. You don't have to take on their energy or worry about the outcome. When you align with your own source of power and love, you extend kindness to others. Let others do and say what they wish. It is part of their own journey and plan. Recognize everyone has their own time and place in life.

• • •

I am comfortable with my self and fully present in the moment of my life. I allow others to be who they are without my need to try to change them. I have loving kindness for all and allowance for others to be in their own place in life. I have compassion for myself and accept my own place in my own journey as well. For today, I am right where I need to be.

• • •

What relationship do I struggle with the most?
How can I allow that person to be true to themselves?

LIFE IS A BALANCING ACT OF HOLDING ON AND LETTING GO.

The art of letting go is a surrendering process guided by love and light. If you grasp onto outcomes, people or situations in fear of losing what you have, you restrict the flow of positivity into your life. Recognize there are chapters of your life, and sometimes people, places and situations are meant to be let go. Know that nothing is ever lost. It will stay in your heart forever.

• • •

I am grateful for everything in my life. I embrace all of life's situations and release situations, people and ideals often. Life is a balancing act of holding on and letting go, and I have mastered this.

• • •

What am I holding onto that wants to be released?

I HONOR MY BODY'S NEEDS.

You body is a vessel for growth and self-reflection. When you listen to its wisdom, you will feel calmer. Your body has needs as well. Take time to honor your body by treating it with kindness and love. Send loving thoughts to it instead of blame and critical energy. Treat it to a massage or luxurious bath. Also spend time moving your body and giving it exercise. Your body craves movement and energy flow. When you exercise, you honor you body's deepest desires.

• • •

My body is a vessel for love. I respect my body by honoring its needs. I move my body with exercise each day and I listen to the wisdom within. My body has protected me, grown with me and allowed me to be present on Earth. I show up fully in my life by treating my body as a friend and guide.

• • •

What is my body craving?

I PUT DOWN THE PITY PARTY.

Release the need to be right and stop blaming others for your own situation. Today is an empowering opportunity for you to take responsibility for your life. You are living a creative adventure and the more present you are, the happier you will be. Instead of being the victim of the harassment of your life, stand tall and move forward with conviction and understanding. You are only as weak as you allow yourself to be. Rather than focusing on what happened and how you may have been wronged, focus on what you learned. Your power lies in how you pick yourself up and move forward.

• • •

I have no shame or worry. I release all fear. I take full responsibility for my life and the role I played in each situation. I stand tall, confidently embracing this next phase of my life. I make powerful choices aligned with my true self. When I retreat inward, I am reminded nothing is out of order or place. Everything that happened helped me learn more about myself. I send love and light to others, including myself.

• • •

Who am I blaming for my misfortune?
Send them love and forgive them.

I AM THE HERO OF MY OWN LIFE STORY.

You have been through so much in your life. You have a choice. You can look at mistakes from you past with regret and throw emotional hate onto others, or you can overcome all of the challenges with love. Everything you have ever experienced is part of a bigger picture.

You have a unique story that is yours to share. You will empower others when you share your real self with others. Just like the hero who has overcome life difficulties, you too will rise above the pain to show your true purpose. You are the hero of you own life. Start showing up as the hero and the overcomer.

• • •

I am the hero of my life's epic journey. I have overcome great difficulties and I have survived the challenges. I am heroic in my nature and accept my power into grace. I stand tall with courage and a dedication to self for the greater good. When I show up for myself, I help others. It is my mission to help and make a difference. I can do this by being true to myself.

• • •

What epic challenge have I overcome?

I CAN BE AND DO ANYTHING I WANT IN THIS LIFE.

Stop listening to what other people say is best for you. The world has its own set of standards and the frustration and angst you feel inside are because you know that won't work for you. You have a unique set of gifts that only you can bring forth in the world. Remove your limiting thoughts and go for your heart's desires. When you lead your life from your heart center, you will be rewarded in every way possible. Show your true self and watch your dreams come true.

• • •

I am connected to my purpose, which is my truth. I have dreams that live inside of me and they deserve to be seen. The world wants me as I am. It is never too late or early to be what I might be. I can do anything and everything I want when I live from my heart.

• • •

What dream have I been ignoring?

IT DIDN'T WORK OUT AND THAT'S A BEAUTIFUL THING.

Perhaps you are focusing a lot of your energy on what might have been. Maybe you pursued a dream and it didn't turn out the way you thought, or a relationship or job recently showed its true colors.

Instead of looking at the situation as a bust or focusing on what didn't work, start celebrating the process and what you learned. Sometimes things are not meant to last, but that doesn't mean they didn't work out. Trust you got exactly what you needed and it is time to move on.

• • •

There is no point in staying in my past. I gave it my best and that is enough. I am happy things didn't work out because I learned more about what I need in this life. I release my attachment to the past and see everything is actually in right order. The situation was exactly what it was, it was never meant to last and that is a beautiful thing.

• • •

What dream did I have to let go of?

I LOVE MY LIFE.

You may be spending a lot of energy focusing on what is not working. This is a natural human tendency. But for today, celebrate all that is well. No matter where you are in your journey to happiness, you have a wonderful life. When you focus on the amazing accomplishments, personal triumphs and beautiful friends around you, you will see how loved and abundant you are. Celebrate your awesome life and focus on the positive aspects.

• • •

I am in love with my life. I smile brightly as I beam with love. Everything in my life is perfect as is. I release all worry and pain because I know I am cared for and loved. My life is beautiful as am I.

• • •

What do I love about my life?

I HAVE ENOUGH TIME, ENERGY AND MONEY FOR WHAT I CARE MOST ABOUT.

You might have goals and dreams but limit yourself because of resources. If you focus on the lack or what you don't have, you will not be able to see the resources available to you. Universal law allows you to get everything you need, but you must focus on what you want, instead of what you don't have or don't want.

The truth is you always have enough time, money and energy for what is most important to you. If it is important enough, you will always find a way.

• • •

I go courageously and confidently in the direction of my dreams. My heart is speaking to me and I listen with attentive focus. I have plenty of resources, time and energy to get what I desire. When I focus on what I want, I will get what I want. I release all lack mentality and turn all my attention to the possibilities of my tomorrow.

• • •

What goal is most important to me right now?
How can I put more time, money or energy into it?

WHEN I AM FEELING ANGST, I ASK, "WHAT IS THIS SITUATION TRYING TO TEACH ME?"

Every situation in your life is an opportunity to learn more about yourself. Instead of resisting or looking at the pain as frustration, turn inward and ask what you can learn here. The lessons available to you will help you move through the situation with more grace.

. . .

Every situation I am in is an opportunity to learn. I grow into my true self by diving into the lessons. I remove fear as I step forward with confidence and purpose. I retreat to my heart and allow my inner voice to show me the truth of all situations. I am open to learning.

. . .

What can I learn from this pain?

I'M GRATEFUL FOR MY HEALTH.

When you are sick, you may recognize how important your health is. But when you are well, you most likely expect your body to work and give little attention to the positive aspects of being healthy. Today, focus on your health and celebrate your well-being. Your health is an important aspect in your overall happiness. When you can send love to yourself and be thankful for feeling well, you maintain positive spirits.

• • •

I am grateful for my health. I focus on the good in my life and positive intentions. I am well and full of life. My lifestyle is conducive to health and a beacon of love. I choose foods that make me feel energetic and healthy. I detox my body when I feel it is time and I embrace my happy and healthy body. I am grateful for my health.

• • •

How can I celebrate my health?

I ACKNOWLEDGE MY DISCOMFORTS.

Your body has a message for you. When you are in pain or discomfort, it is not something to ignore or resist. Instead of looking at the discomfort as painful, look at it as purpose. There is purpose to all discomfort in your body. When you go inward and ask why you are hurting, your inner knowing will reveal the truth. All discomfort in your body and life are an opportunity to look at what is not working.

• • •

I acknowledge my discomforts by sending each one love and light. I release the pain and trust it will be removed from my life. The pain I feel is part of my past and I no longer resonate with it. I can learn from all body aches and discomforts. As I seek the truth, I am revealed opportunity for expansion.

• • •

What discomfort can I embrace?

I AM NOT DISAPPOINTED WITH MYSELF.

Watch your words and what you are projecting out into the world. You may feel disappointment and pain from your past, but carrying that extra burden hurts your ability to move forward. Forgive yourself for anything you have done to yourself that you worry was wrong. Negative habits, insecurities and fear-based thoughts can disappear when you forgive yourself.

• • •

I am not mad at myself for anything that has happened. I let go of holding onto the guilt and release my attachment to the pain. I am not disappointed, for everything I have ever done is part of my greater understanding of my life. I actively look inward to see what each situation can teach me. I am at peace with where I am in my life.

• • •

What recent situation do I blame myself for?

IT'S GO TIME.

Stop procrastinating and go for it. You are capable of reaching your desired outcome and more equipped than you realize. You have everything you need inside of you. You just need to take action forward. Use all of your energy and insight to move the situation or project into full focus. It is go time and you are in a place to accomplish great things. Believe in yourself and you will succeed.

• • •

I am motivated and inspired to move forward with my creative ideas. I am connected to my purpose, which means the momentum is working with me to achieve my desired outcome. I work swiftly and focus on my dreams with clear action and insight.

• • •

What can I start today?

I DON'T HAVE TO MOVE ON TO LET GO.

You may be feeling at a loss with a recent event or the closing down of a relationship, situation or dream. The universe might be nudging you to move on and let go, but you're feeling conflicted. If you are navigating a broken heart, you can retreat into your heart for guidance. Your heart will lead you to let go and this is different than moving on.

You can emotional forgive and release relationships, situations or dreams by letting go of the outcome. When it is time to move on, you will know. You don't have to rush or force anything.

• • •

I am okay with where I am today, as I know I am right where I need to be. I don't force anything in my life, including relationships, situations or dreams. I balance the art of letting go with moving on. I trust I don't have to move on but I can emotionally release the energetic hold of each troubling situation.

• • •

What have I been trying to let go of but can't move on from?

I DON'T NEED PERMISSION TO DO WHAT FEELS RIGHT.

You have a unique internal compass that is special to you. When you try to do what others think is right, you fail to follow through on what is right for you. Instead of seeking approval from others or running all your ideas by everyone, turn to your heart and connect with the energy of love. Let love move you forward and you will become a beacon of hope for others. Your light will shine and you will be doing what feels right for you.

• • •

I don't need others' permission to do what feels right for me. I trust myself and my dreams and ideas are important. I honor myself by listening to my heart and following through on action.

• • •

Where can I stop second-guessing my own judgment?

I REFUSE TO TAKE NO FOR AN ANSWER.

When others tell you no, it is not a forever state. No is temporary. It is up to you to decide if you will keep going or surrender. If you are working toward a dream, others may try to chime in on your path and tell you it can't be done.

You have no need for negativity on your mission to happy. Instead of listening to them, keep going. When you are connected to your heart, you are living on purpose. And if the dream is in your heart, it matters. You belong in this world and so do your dreams.

• • •

If someone tells me it can't be done, I say, "Watch me." I am powerful and capable of achieving glorious things in this life. "Bring it on" is my mantra as I embrace the journey and move forward with my dreams. No one can stop me but me. I refuse to let negative energy into my life. I surround myself with supportive energy and love. My dreams are coming true.

• • •

Where have I allowed "no" to stop me?

I AM THE KINDEST PERSON I KNOW.

Kindness is the best way for you to navigate through any difficult situation involving another person. Being kind will help you seek the truth of all matters. When others offend you or stab you with words, you don't need to take on their harmful intentions. Simply connect back to yourself and align with your inner light. You can forgive them and send them kindness and love.

• • •

I am kind. I choose not to associate with fear-based thoughts or attacks from other people. Instead of judging others for their actions, I hold my internal strength by aligning with kindness and peace. All is well in the world when I show my true self, the kind, loving, peaceful person I know I am.

• • •

What act of kindness can I do right now?

I REFRAIN FROM CORRECTING OTHERS.

You may want to communicate clearly with those around you, but pay attention anytime you interrupt or correct them. This can often alienate conversations and keep you from being heard. When you overshadow others in conversation, you may be trying to be noticed. Instead of finishing others' sentences or interrupting to correct them, look inward to yourself and see if you can give yourself approval and self-care. When you pay attention to yourself and your needs, you will feel no need to overshadow others.

• • •

I am aligned with my authentic self. This means I honor my needs and act on my desires. I communicate with others by listening intently to what they have to say. I refrain from overshadowing conversations by interrupting or steering them to fit my own needs. I respect the time and attention of others by communicating clearly and with integrity.

• • •

Where do I overshadow or dominate conversations?

I HONOR MY COMMITMENTS.

Honoring yourself means you honor your commitments to others and yourself. When was the last time you broke a promise to yourself or another person? When you say you are going to do something and you don't, you break promises to yourself. When this happens, you build up energetic walls that harm your self-confidence. To empower yourself, forgive yourself for all past broken promises and commit to your commitments moving forward.

• • •

I am committed to living a life of integrity. I am honest with myself and I honor all commitments. When I make a promise to myself and others, I always follow through. I value my words. I place power in the commitments I make.

• • •

What promise can I keep to myself?

TIME IS ON MY SIDE.

You may feel pressed for time and deadlines may be in your face, but time can expand for you. When you add more joy into what you do, you will have unlimited time and potential. If you are stressed out because you are trying to meet a deadline, consider a more playful way through the process.

If you are powering through it, you may be missing the point. Adding more playful energy will help you be more productive as well. The more fun you have, the more successful you will be.

• • •

Time is nothing but an illusion. There is no time, only space. I stand powerfully in this moment accepting all that I am. I have endless amounts of time in front of me and I meet all my demands. I add more joy into everything I do and time expands.

• • •

When do I lose myself in the moment and forget about time?

REAL LOVE IS UNCONDITIONAL AND NEVER ENDS.

You don't have to be so hard on yourself. The relationship that ended will forever be part of you because it lives in your heart. When others tell you to move on, you may feel burdened with pressure. But your soul knows there is nothing to move on from. Real love never dies. It will always live in your heart. The situation and experience may change form, but you will forever and always be connected in your hearts.

• • •

I am connected in my life to my heart. Real love never fades, it just changes form. I embrace the journey of life as some love changes shape, but it never changes in my heart. Love is love and that is all there is.

• • •

Who have I been forcing myself to get over? Let love lead the way.

I AM NEVER STUCK. THERE IS ALWAYS SOMETHING I CAN DO.

You are only trapped by your thoughts. You are never stuck. Catch yourself if you say, "I don't have a choice," or "I had to do it." That is a mindset stuck in entrapment. The feeling of being trapped is inspired by a lack of love.

Your fear may be running the show. Instead of listening to your fear, focus inward and let your heart lead the way. Your heart will show you that you are never trapped, you always have a choice, and which action you can take to move out of all troubling situations.

• • •

I listen to my heart in all situations. I am never trapped or stuck. I can always do something to help free me of the pain. I focus on my heart's intentions, for it will lead me through any darkness. I let it lead the way.

• • •

Where do I feel trapped?
What step can I take to remove myself from the situation?

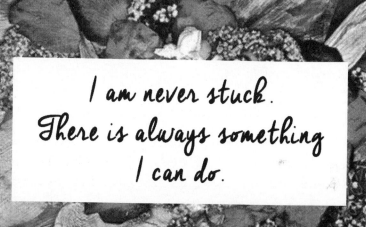

I am never stuck.
There is always something
I can do.

I FEEL ABUNDANT AND LIVE A RICH LIFE NOW.

You don't have to wait for financial abundance to have fun. When you focus on the rich rewards of your current, life you will attract more abundance to you. If you are waiting on happiness by saying things like, "I will do that when I have more money," or "I will be happy when things fall into place," you are keeping yourself from your true desires. Instead, find ways to give yourself the security, abundance and love you seek. You will become happier and abundance will flow to you.

• • •

I am abundant. I am full of joy. I am living a rich life now. I connect to my inner desires and align them with love. I seek support from the universe by allowing abundance to flow to me. I am connected to my life and I live in joy.

• • •

How can I cultivate abundance in this moment?

I HAVE THE COURAGE TO BECOME WHO I AM MEANT TO BE.

It isn't who you are holding you back. It might be who you think you aren't. Instead of listening to your fears and insecurities, focus on who your really are. Honor your strengths and share your talents with the world. Have courage to be true to yourself. It is the greatest gift of all.

• • •

I am courageous with my life. I show the world who I really am with confidence. I like who I have become and every day I am becoming more of who I am supposed to be. I honor myself by showing the world my true colors. I am courageous with my life. I am becoming who I am meant to be.

• • •

Where can I be more courageous with my heart?

JUST BECAUSE IT HASN'T BEEN DONE DOESN'T MEAN IT CAN'T.

Society puts a lot of pressure on you. To be and do things differently than you want. You may have a goal or dream inside your heart, but it has never been done before. There is no need to abandon your dream. The fact that it has never been done gives you leeway to create the path forward.

Because it hasn't been done before means you get to write the rule book. If you are honest with yourself, you will seek your truth. And you have dreams that yearn to manifest. So despite the conditions of the world, go for it.

• • •

I can do it. I am able to achieve greatness. The world is my playground and I joyfully leap through all obstacles. I am a force of energy and focus. When I put my mind to something I desire, it will come true. My head and heart are aligned and I courageously carve out new territory for my dreams to come true.

• • •

What have I always wanted to do that has never been done?

I AM COMPASSIONATE.

Being kind to others can be a challenge if you don't understand where they are coming from. Maybe they said something that hurt your feelings or reacted to you in an unexpected way. No matter what the situation, turning to compassion will help you overcome all difficulties. If you seek out understanding in others, you will find truth and awareness.

• • •

I am compassionate and see all situations with love. I may not understand others' motives, but I am willing to empathize with them. I am kind and loving to all who I meet and I compassionately show my intentions with love.

• • •

Where can I be more understanding?

I TAKE RESPONSIBILITY FOR MY HAPPINESS.

You are doing a phenomenal job at life. No one gave you a manual on how to live a happy life. You have to seek it and carve out joy for yourself. You already know no one can make you happy but yourself. And you are showing up for yourself by reading books, taking courses and following your heart's guidance. Happiness is a moment-by-moment experience; it's not just a destination but rather a way of life. Happiness is a mindset you cultivate the moment you choose to be happy.

• • •

I am happy. I make a choice to be positive and see the good in my life. My happiness is not outside of me. It is inside of me and I connect with it daily. I am in joy and I am full of love.

• • •

How can I take more responsibility for my joy?

THE GRASS IS GREENEST WHERE I STAND.

Looking outside of yourself for happiness is preventing you from feeling the pure joy in this moment. When you seek happiness in places, things, people or experiences, they may elude you. The grass is not greener over there.

You may see evidence of this in your life as you explore new situations, hoping they will make you happy, only to find yourself stuck, sad and depressed. This happens because people try to fix problems by escaping them. But the problem will always persist until you water the grass where you stand. Focus on solving your current problems before you run away from them.

• • •

I am present in my life and that means I water the grass I stand on. I know that no matter where I go, there I am, which means my problems, solutions and grievances will never disappear until I address them directly. I choose to compassionately solve all situations in my life and I move effortlessly through transitions.

• • •

What problem can I focus on fixing?

I DON'T WAIT IN VAIN.

If you are waiting for an answer or you want more clarity, focus all your attention on what you want. Don't give any energy to what you don't want. Your thoughts create your outcome. Hold faith. If you let your fears take over your thoughts, you will feel emotional pain. You don't have to wait in vain for an answer.

Instead of being at the mercy of what others can give you, send love to the situation and ask the universe, your guides or higher power for support. Trust the situation will work out in your favor.

• • •

Everything is unfolding perfectly and I get what I want. The universe is helping me become more of who I really am by giving me what I really need in life. I ask for what I want and I wait patiently with love to receive my desires. When I am confident of the outcome, I wait without worry.

• • •

What situation am I waiting on?
How can I add more life into the situation?

I DON'T KEEP SCORE.

Refrain from trying to one-up those around you. When you try to keep score, you damage your own potential for reaching your desires. By focusing on what others are or are not doing, you take attention off of yourself and your life's plan. Focus your attention back on your own desires and let go of trying to keep score.

• • •

I do not judge others' actions or keep track of their mistakes. I am aligned with this moment of my life and I stay present for all situations. It is not a race, nor do I need to try to one-up another person. I am aligned with my own self, which means I have nothing to keep score of.

• • •

What scorecard can I erase?

MONEY WILL ALWAYS FLOW. MY SOURCE OF ABUNDANCE IS DIVINE.

If you are worried about finances, recognize where your fear is coming from. Do you have a lack mentality or believe there isn't enough? Some of the fears you carry might come from your parents. When we can look at our lack mentality and fears around scarcity, we can reverse them by focusing on the truth. The universe is abundant and plentiful, so turn your attention to the opportunities instead of lack.

• • •

I am always provided for because the universe has an infinite amount of resources. There is plenty to go around. I release all my concern around lack of money and support. I am cared for and I always have what I need.

• • •

Where has scarcity or lack-based thought prevented me from doing what I love?

I AM EXTRAORDINARY.

You are not giving yourself enough credit. You are far too hard on your own self. If you could see yourself the way others do, you would be amazed. That little blemish, odd body part or quirky characteristic is part of what makes you special. Start beating the drum of how fabulous you are and let go of insecurity and all self-blame.

• • •

I am amazing. I am capable of extraordinary things. When I put my mind to anything, I can accomplish it. I know I am my own biggest critic and today I breakup with my self-blame. There is nothing wrong with me. There is nothing to fix. I am extraordinary. I make a difference in everyone's lives because I am gift to this world.

• • •

How can I celebrate my awesome self?

I SHARE MY INSIGHTS OPENLY WITH OTHERS.

You may have great ideas but are afraid to share them with others. Pay attention to your conversations and see how you feel when it is your time to share your truth. When you align with your heart center and speak with experience, you will feel confident and be open to expressing your honest voice. Be proud of yourself and your ideas. They matter.

• • •

I am free to express my opinion and share openly with others. When I have an idea or comment, I speak up with integrity and purpose. I am confident as I show my expressive nature. Others respond to my ideas in a positive way because I am expressing my true self.

• • •

Where can I speak up?

I SIMPLIFY MY ENTIRE LIFE.

Clutter is a byproduct of indecision. Look around you. Is your environment cluttered? When you take time to de-clutter and reorganize your belongings, you will feel more balanced. You will feel more productive as you invite fresh opportunistic energy in. When you eliminate clutter from your home and work place, you balance the flow of energy.

• • •

I am clutter free. My workspace and personal environment are reflections of my personal position in life. I simplify and remove all necessary and unwanted things. When I keep a clean and clutter-free space, I respect myself and my home. I eliminate extra stuff so I can balance my life.

• • •

What can I remove from my life right now?

I AM AN OUTSTANDING LISTENER.

Listen closely to the pulse of your heart. A gentle beating and constant stir is within you. When you close your eyes, you will feel desires in motion. If you spend a lot of time in the chaos and noise of life, today is a reminder to get quiet. Listen to others without interruption or trying to fix them and give yourself permission to listen to yourself. When you quiet the mind, you can hear your heart.

• • •

I listen with my heart. I am present in my life and in all conversations. I communicate with others by being an outstanding listener. I hold space for others to share their stories and life with me. I respond by listening, there is no need to speak or interrupt.

My ears are a valuable tool to help me manifest my own desires. I retreat inward and listen to my heart and the direction it whispers to me. I am connected to my source of love and light and I listen to the universe's guidance.

• • •

When I listen to my heart what does it say?

I AM GENTLE WITH MYSELF IN TRANSITIONS.

Moving from one phase of your life into the next can feel unnerving. When you navigate transitions, there is a period of great change. This drastic energy may feel scary but you have nothing to fear. The fear of the unknown is just a lack of clarity. You can remove this fear by focusing on what you want and taking action toward your goals. Through any transition, be compassionate and patient with yourself. You are growing. Much like the caterpillar that becomes a butterfly, you are getting ready to spread your own wings.

• • •

I am kind and compassionate with myself through all phases of my life. When I am in transition, I pay extra attention to my needs and I serve myself by listening to my inner voice. When I fall into fear, I return back to my own true self, which will show me the next right action to take. Transitions are a joyful experience, as I know I am growing and becoming more of who I am supposed to be.

• • •

What change am I going through where I could use more gentle support?

I TAKE A LEAP OF FAITH.

Having faith will serve you well right now. You may have a goal or dream and be unsure of how to proceed. First you must believe in yourself and hold faith that it is possible. When you lead from your heart, you will be guided with love. Take a leap and move forward with your dreams. Taking a leap of faith also relates to a new relationship and romantic love. If you are unsure of your path forward, trust your heart and jump into the experience.

• • •

I remove all fear of the unknown and I comfortably take a leap into my future. I am being guided with love and the universe supports my desires. There is nothing to fear for all is in right order.

• • •

Where can I take a leap of faith?

MY LIFE GETS BETTER WHEN I PUSH THROUGH MY COMFORT ZONE.

What have you always wanted to do but have yet to give a go? Your comfort zone may need some stretching. You might be comfortable doing things a specific way and a routine can feel safe and predictable. But stepping out of your comfort zone will bring fresh life and energy into your routine. Revisit your dreams from childhood days. What have you always wanted to do? Now is the time to go for it.

• • •

I embrace new opportunities with excitement and wonder. I follow through on my dreams by stepping out of my current routine. I step out of my comfort zone which helps me grow and change. My dreams matter and I go after them with gusto.

• • •

Where can I stop playing it safe?

ALL MY FEARS ARE FANTASY.

When you listen to your fears, your life may feel unmanageable. When we let fear run the show, it creates false illusions and separates you from others. Fear is based on stories in your mind that can harm you and others. Fear clouds your judgment ands prevents you from making smart choices. To recognize your fear say, "My fear is not real, I choose love."

• • •

When I pay attention to my fears, they create new realities for me. I choose to disengage from all fear-based thoughts and I return to love. Love will guide me into my real dream life, one guided by support and positive action.

• • •

What fear do I believe that is most outrageous?

I TAKE A DEEP BREATH AND I LET GO.

Breathe in deeply and feel the energy flood through your body. You may be stressed out and forget to breathe. Breathing is a natural part of life but holding onto your breath is like holding on and resisting life. It prevents you from moving forward.

The same way you prepare yourself to do something new, speak in front of an audience, sky dive or go on an trip, you take a deep breath and then step forward to go for it. Use this process to step into the unknown. You may be holding onto a situation that wants to be released. Take a deep breath and let go.

• • •

I am focused on my big picture. I know when to let go and stop pushing to make things happen. When fear steps in, I breathe deeply into my body and release the worry. I replace all fear with love as I confidently step forward into the next phase of my life. I take a breath and I let go.

• • •

What can I dive into?

FOLLOWING MY HEART IS THE MOST RESPONSIBLE THING I CAN DO FOR MY WELL-BEING.

How well do you feel? Gauging your wellness by how often you listen to your heart is a process you can cultivate. Your heart is a tool to help you feel and do your best.

When you look at your life and see the things you enjoy and appreciate, it's evidence your heart has been in the driver's seat of your decisions. If you look around and see situations you dislike, you can take responsibility for your own happiness and health and listen to your heart.

• • •

I listen to my heart one hundred percent of the time. I gauge my wellness by how much happiness I feel in my life. When I am happy, it is a reflection of my heart leading the way. I choose happiness, health and wellness and this comes from me listening to my heart.

• • •

How can I be more responsible for my own well-being?

EVEN THE DARKNESS HAS ITS WONDERS.

There is beauty in the breakdown. If you are depressed or in a desperate place, wonder can be found in the moment. Go into the situation and feel the emotions fully. Part of living a rich life is to feel each moment and accept what it offers. When you embrace the darkness, the light will come. Ask yourself what you can learn here and why you are experiencing this. Your inner voice will lead you through the darkness.

• • •

I can see the light. Even in my darkest hour, I reach for hope. This helps me pull into a place of understanding and peace. I can overcome anything when I am present and focused. I rise above this pain to see the purpose. There is wonder in every moment of my life. I am present for the experience.

• • •

What purpose can I see in my current pain?

I AM EITHER IN A YEAR OF STUDY OR SHARING.

Your life does not have to be a constant state of expansion. It has ebbs and flows, just like the tides in the ocean. Pay attention to your situation and see what pattern you are in. Some years you will experience great learning and deep study. This can be a brilliant time to read more books, take new courses or go back to school. You may also study experiences, such as lessons in love, forgiveness and faith. When you ask questions, you will always receive the answers.

Some years, you may be in more of an outward expression of self. This is a time of great wonder as you explore life and express your deep understanding and lessons learned.

• • •

Years of my life are divided. Some years I ask questions, others I get answers. I embrace the journey and connect with my life's purpose. I understand my life is a reflection of my learning. Some years, I experience great depth of inward study and others I share openly and express myself to the world. I fully accept my life as a creative adventure and deep study.

• • •

Am I in a year of study or sharing?

DEPRESSION IS A LADDER.

You may feel stuck or consumed with depression. If this is your current experience, you can celebrate, for there is light at the end of this dark tunnel. Depression is an opening into our soul and your true desires. Depression is a probing of what needs to be changed in your life. Look at the situation with a focus on getting out. Use the depression to climb your way into new awareness of yourself and your life.

• • •

I am not my depression. It does not consume me. I can use my low energy to improve my life. My feelings are my compass pointing me into a direction of greater understanding of myself and the choices I made. I look inward at my true desires and climb my way out of my depression.

• • •

What is my depression trying to show me?

I DO WHAT WORKS.

You do what works for you because there is a reward and payoff. Even your destructive, self-sabotaging behaviors have a reward. You do them because you get a payoff. If there was no value, you would quit.

If you want to break a habit or stop an addiction, identify your reward and look at the real payoff. You have to create a new reward system, which will give you new results.

• • •

I shape my own behaviors by the payoffs I receive in life. When I want to change habits or quit addictions, I find control by examining my payoff. I can control my outcome by refocusing my behavior and reward system. I do what works for me. If what once worked no longer brings me joy, I look at the payoff and find a new rewards system.

• • •

What payoff is no longer pleasing me?

I CAN REINVENT MYSELF AT ANY TIME.

It is never too late to be what you wanted for yourself. You can change directions and start fresh at any time. Part of the joy of life is expressing yourself and trying new things. If your heart is calling you to change careers, try a new hair color or move to a new country, follow this impulse. It is not rash or inappropriate. It is your mission. That constant feeling that something is missing will disappear when you give yourself permission to reinvent yourself and try new things.

• • •

I have ideas dear to my heart. I confidently express these ideas and share them with the world. It is always the right time to change course and try new things. I experience my life fully, which means I dive into all of my heart's callings with positive energy and a willingness to succeed.

• • •

How can I reinvent myself?

THERE IS ONLY ONE ME.

You may feel lonely because you are trying to fit in. You are not made to fit in. You are unique and special as you are. Pay attention to your thoughts about other people as well. Do you compare yourself to others? When you look at others in reflection to your own life, you may think they have more or are more successful than you. When you compare yourself to others, it separates you from love. It also prevents you from feeling your true worth. Instead of looking at others and comparing them to yourself, focus on how unique you are.

• • •

I am special and unique as I am. It does not serve me to compare myself to other people because everyone is special in their own unique way. I want to be me and have no desire to be like anyone else. My life is my own to create, so I actively celebrate myself and all I can do.

• • •

Who can I stop comparing myself too?

I DO ONE THING EVERYDAY MY FUTURE SELF WILL HUG ME FOR.

You are in control of your life and the outcome. Yes, there is a balance of fate and freewill, but if you sit back and let life happen to you, you will miss opportunities for you to become what you desire. Instead of waiting on happiness or for things to fall into place, start to action out a plan for your life. Create a big picture goal and do at least one thing everyday your future self will hug you for.

• • •

I embrace my life as a creative endeavor. I jump in with both feet. I do not wait for happiness. I go out and create my life adventure. I show up for my future self by taking steps today to get me where I want to go. I am in control of my life.

• • •

What action step can I take today that
my future self will hug me for?

I AVOID DEAD-END CONVERSATIONS. INSTEAD I TALK ABOUT MY DREAMS AND GOALS.

Gossip is contagious and can be a source of conversation, especially when you are bored or trying to fit in. If others are engaging in conversations that make you feel frustrated, alienated or bored, it is up to you to exit. You need not stay in any situation, including conversation, that is a waste of your time. Avoid dead-end conversation by talking about your goals and dreams.

• • •

Time is my most precious resource. I do not waste it. I am aligned with my purpose and I focus my intentions with love and light. When I speak with others, I am intentional in my communication and do not waste it by engaging in conversation that does not serve my intention. I talk about my goals and dreams and support those who do as well.

• • •

Who can I disengage with and stop wasting
time in dead-end conversations?

I AM CONFIDENT IN BELIEFS THAT WORK FOR ME.

Others may have conflicted beliefs or opinions. This may cause stress or arguments. There is nothing to change about other people who have contrasting opinions. The contrast of life is what makes it rewarding. Without other people's point of view, you would not understand your own so clearly. Instead of turning to arguments or judgment, align with your own beliefs and why you feel the way you do.

You don't need to prove other people wrong. When you are comfortable with what you stand for, you can become an example of your views. You don't need to tell people what you care about. You can show them.

• • •

I refuse to argue my beliefs in order to get others to believe me. I am confident in my understanding of self and all I stand for. The beliefs that work for me are part of my own rewarding journey and I respect that others have their own path. I connect with my own sense of self by showing people what I care about instead of telling them.

• • •

What can I show people instead of telling them?

I TRY MY DREAMS OUT.

Is there a goal in your heart that has yet to become a reality? Dreams come to you for a reason. If you give yourself permission to try your dream, you will never live in regret or fear. Living a full, rich life means you go for what matters to you. It is perfectly okay to try your dreams. Maybe rent the house before you buy, or move to Hawaii for a season before you move permanently. What goal in your heart can you try?

The goal in your heart wants to be explored. As you get into your dreams and start living them, you will learn more about them. Sometimes dreams are meant to be explored but not permanently part of your life. Allow yourself to try your dreams.

• • •

I live a full and happy life because I explore my heart's desires. My dreams come to me for a reason and I make them come true by taking steps forward to live them. I release my attachment to things working out and instead appreciate the journey of discovery. I learn more about myself through each dream I try. I live a no regrets lifestyle because my life is full of love and I am living from my heart.

• • •

What dream can I try?

NO ONE ELSE KNOWS WHAT'S BEST FOR ME.

Have you been second-guessing yourself or asking other people for their opinions about your life? Ask yourself if this is serving you. When we ask others for their opinions, it is because we are unsure. But when we get to the heart of the situation, we always know what is best for ourselves. No one else knows how you should live your life. Do yourself a favor and stop trusting everyone else's opinion. Instead trust your own.

• • •

I trust myself and listen to my inner voice. I do not need to ask others for advice because I know what is right for me. I trust my own guidance and listen to it with an open mind. I know what is best for me. My heart is my compass.

• • •

What advice have I recently received from another person when I already knew the answer?

WHAT I SEE IN OTHERS IS A REFLECTION OF MYSELF.

When you look at others with judgment, you are judging yourself. What we see in others is a reflection of our own position in life. Instead of reacting or blaming others, ask yourself what each situation brings up for you. If another person is rude, but you feel you are kind, ask yourself where you are rude in your life. You may be surprised to find you are disrespectful and talk down to yourself. When you are accountable for your reflections, you can align with love and positive light.

• • •

I am accountable for all my feelings. Instead of attacking others, I look inward with curiosity. I know I am a mirror for others and what I dislike about them is something within myself that needs attention. I can choose to see what I see in others, and I focus on the good. I cultivate more loving relationships being kind and compassionate to myself first.

• • •

What person bothers me, and how is this a reflection of myself?

WHEN I LOOK AT THE WORLD AS A GOOD, HAPPY AND KIND PLACE, GOOD, HAPPY AND KIND THINGS COME TO ME.

Your experience of the world is largely affected by how you see the world. You will empower yourself by focusing on what you want to see and experience. Look at what you believe in and see if that is reflected in your life. Focus your energy into feeling positive thoughts and believe the world is on your side.

When you believe people and the world are good, you will see evidence of this in your everyday life. Happiness comes to those who open up to seeing happiness possible for them.

• • •

I deserve to be happy and healthy. I am kind and loving and do everything with great love. I make choices from a loving place and I give others the benefit of the doubt. I believe in the greater good of mankind and I am part of peace. When I show up happy, kind and from a good feeling place, this is reflected in every experience of my life.

• • •

What kind loving thoughts can I project out into the world?

I AM WORTH IT AND I HAVE A LOT TO GIVE.

You have so much to give this world and other people. When you share your opinions, views, ideas and self with others, with vulnerability and honesty, people fall in love with you. The more true to yourself you are, the more others can get to know you. If you only show a side of you that is *a version of what you think they want to see,* you do yourself and others a disservice. By being true to yourself, you give the true you to the world. You share an honest reflection of yourself, which invites authentic connections into your life.

• • •

I am true to myself by being my real self. I don't hide behind masks or false versions of me. I am proud and confident of who I have become. I am worth it and I have a lot to give this world. My ideas are respected and I am admired for my transparency.

• • •

Where can I give more of my real self?

THE REAL FAILURE IS TRYING TO PLEASE EVERYONE.

If you feel tired and worn out, it could be a reflection of how much you are trying to please others. If you spend your time trying to get approval and support from others, you will be running yourself in circles. Trying to be there for everyone all the time has not served you in the past.

Instead of over-extending yourself, learn the power of no. By saying no to situations, you preserve your energy and align with your own truth. Focus your energy into activities and situations that bring you joy. When you show up for your passions, you give yourself the gift of self-love. When you are kind and loving to yourself, you are able to be there for others more fully.

• • •

I am passionate about my endeavors and hobbies. I pursue my passions with excitement and joy. When I show up for me, there is no one to answer to. I can connect with myself and preserve my energy by doing what makes me happy. I release my need to please everyone and start pleasing myself. My needs matter and I put myself first.

• • •

What act of self-care can I do today?

My life gets
better by change,
not chance.

MY LIFE GETS BETTER BY CHANGE, NOT CHANCE.

People make changes in their lives for two reasons. Change is either inspired by fear and desperation, or by inspiration. When you make choices from a heartfelt place, you will grow into new beginnings with love and grace. If you make changes out of fear, you are still cultivating new experiences and growth opportunities, but the energy may feel more challenging. No matter what, your life gets better through active change.

You can wait for your life circumstances to change, but this does not happen by chance. Everything you have ever done in your life is part of an orchestrated plan. You get to conduct your masterpiece. When you put everything you have learned into play, you create deep, rich experiences that reward your soul. Change in your life comes from you taking action.

• • •

I make calculate moves forward in my life to create positive change. My life is ever-changing and I am in flow. I embrace change as though I have chosen it myself, because I have. Everything I experience is my choice and I choose to make choices from inspiration and love.

• • •

What change can I make today?

KINDNESS WINS.

Don't take offense to what others say and do. When people hurt you, choose kindness. When people love you, choose kindness. Kindness will always win.

Be authentic with your expression of truth. This means choosing kindness is an option for all who seek internal love. If you are kind to your enemies and you mean it, you will feel more love in your life. Kindness is not something you want to force or pretend. Smiling when you don't feel it is not the act of a kind heart. When you live your life by embracing love, kindness will naturally be your way of life.

• • •

I am kind in the face of negativity. I choose my battles and that helps me overcome all challenges. I do not engage in negative activity and I release all judgment of others. I demonstrate peace by showing the world my kindness. I live from my heart, which is peace and love. I am kind. Kindness wins.

• • •

Who can I be more kind too?

OTHERS CAN'T HURT ME. I CAN ONLY HURT MYSELF.

Don't give your power away to others by allowing them to hurt you. When you allow negative energy into your life, it can prevent you from feeling your true worth. Holding onto negative remarks, opinions or points of view will only hurt you. Release the negativity by turning your attention to positive intentions. When you seek to hold love for yourself, hurtful energy will not come into your life. Others will have no power over you because you will be focused on your true worth and loving yourself.

• • •

I do not allow others to hurt me. I am confident and proud of who I am, which means I stand up for myself in the face of adversity. I choose kindness, love and peace for others and myself. By holding onto negative comments, I understand I am hurting myself, which serves no one. I release negative energy and turn my attention to love.

• • •

What negative comment can I stop replaying in my mind?

I DISENGAGE FROM ALL HARMFUL ACTIVITIES.

If you are going through a difficult situation, you might be trying to cope. It is natural for humans to turn to harmful substances, habits or addictions to help ease the burden of pain. Instead of blaming yourself or feeling guilty for turning to habits or activities that seem bad, embrace your true self with love.

When you can love yourself even through your pain, it will be easier to disengage from harmful activities, people and places. Do all things with love and you will be guided to recover more naturally.

• • •

I am not my addictions or harmful habits. I choose to see myself in a temporary situation and I release my need to numb myself through pain. I disengage from harmful people, places and things by choosing love and letting love guide the way.

• • •

What harmful activity can I stop doing?

I AM READY TO CHANGE AND EMBRACE NEW PATTERNS AND WAYS OF BEING.

Part of life change is willingly accepting change as you embrace new ways of living. Today is a fresh start and an opportunity for you to release old patterns, habits or thoughts that keep bringing you down. Set yourself up for success by creating a focused intention to help you step into the next phase of your life. Stay positive and focus on what you want.

• • •

I am ready for change. I embrace new opportunities and am ready for growth. My life is constantly changing and my journey is unfolding perfectly. I let go of what no longer resonates with me and I step into my future with a positive intention and loving heart.

• • •

What new habit can I start?

EVERY SITUATION IS AN OPPORTUNITY TO CHOOSE LOVE OVER FEAR.

You always have a choice, in every situation. You can choose love or you can choose fear. When you choose fear, you will feel constricted, anxious, overwhelmed, depressed and even angry. If you embrace love, you will feel expansive, hopeful, happy and at peace. Pay attention to how you feel. It will show you the way.

• • •

I choose love in every situation of my life. I embrace the expansive nature of my true self and lead my life from my heart. When I am in fear, I turn to love by expressing my truth. I examine my fear and release it with compassion and love. I always choose love.

• • •

What fear can I replace with love?

MY LIFE IS AN INCREDIBLE JOURNEY.

Have you been focusing on a specific destination? You might be working hard to make situations fall into place but have yet to reach your destination. Take a step back and see how far you have come. Your life is an incredible journey, not a destination.

• • •

My life is a perfect experiment of awe and wonder. I am like a canvas and I get to create my own masterpiece. The masterpiece is not the answer, it is the creative exploration and process. My life is a process and a journey of incredible opportunities. I look at each experience with an open mind and dive into it fully.

• • •

What incredible moment have I recently experienced?

THE MORE I PRACTICE HAPPINESS, THE EASIER IT BECOMES.

Just like exercising at a gym, you can work your happiness muscles. You may be sore are first, but this is a sign of growing strength. Keep going and happiness will be your permanent way of life.

Happiness is something you can wake up with. It is a habit. You can practice happiness by cultivating more self-compassion and love. Self-awareness is the key to connecting you to all you desire. When you practice happiness, it become easier.

• • •

I choose happiness as my way of life. I release my desire to get happy and allow myself to be happy. I am happy already and I have everything I need. There is no need to resist the joy, for I am shining by example.

• • •

What areas of my life have become easier
now that I practice happiness?

LOVE IS THE KEY TO MY SUCCESS.

Love is the key to your success and desires. When you approach your life with love, you will see reflections of all you desire on its way to you. The universe is full of loving support to guide you to your true purpose. When you do everything with love, you will shine brightly for the world to see your true light. Love has no bounds, no enemies and no borders. Choose love and make it an everyday part of life.

• • •

I am love. Everything I do is an indication of my love for myself and the world. I am connected to my world by showing love in each moment. I have no shame or judgment, no denial or self-doubt. Love is all there is. Love is all there will ever be. I am love. I do all things with great love.

• • •

What small thing can I add great love too?

I PAUSE IN MY PLEASURE.

You may feel as though you are alive but not really living. Perhaps you are going through the motions and not engaged with your life. One way to dive deeper into your life and feel the love is to pause in the pleasure. Each day offers abundant opportunities for you to feel joy and passion.

Whether it is eating a fresh orange, drinking your morning latte, driving with your windows down or hugging your dear friend, pleasurable moments happen all the time. When you can pause in each moment, your life becomes more rich and rewarding. Challenge yourself to pause and soak in what life has to offer.

• • •

Taking time to be in each moment of my life will expand my happiness infinitely. I pause in the moments that offer me great pleasure. My life is enriched with multiple rewards. I am present, focused and alive. I pause and take great pleasure in the simple joys of my life.

• • •

What pleasure can I pause in?

REGRETS ARE OPPORTUNITIES TO LEARN AND GROW.

Each experience of your life is an opportunity to learn more about yourself and those around you. When you focus on what went wrong or what might have been, you keep yourself out of the experience of life. When you hold onto regrets, you are causing harm to yourself. It's like saying to yourself, "I made a mistake. I am damaged." But regrets are just areas of our lives that call for more attention. What is it about the situation that caused you frustration or guilt? Go into your regrets and ask what you learned?

• • •

All of my regrets are actually opportunities for growth. I learn from all my regrets by being present in my life. I actively remove my worries by looking at my past and asking myself what I learned. I live a regret-free life because every regret helped me learn more about myself.

• • •

What recent regret have I learned from?

EVERYTHING WILL WORK OUT THE WAY IT SHOULD.

If you feel anxious, you may be worried about the future. Anxieties can cloud your judgment and add more stress to your life. If you were to look back over your life, you may see how in the grand scheme of things everything always works itself out. Instead of worrying about what will or won't happen, focus your attention on what you want to happen. This will help your through the transitions. Everything is in right order and things always fall into place.

• • •

I do not worry about anything. I turn all my fear and anxiety over to the universe and release it for good. I know things work out the way they are supposed to. When I do worry, I quickly turn my attention back to what I want and I am reminded all will work out in my favor.

• • •

What concern will I hand over to the universe?

I DON'T USE AVOIDANCE TACTICS.

Be honest with yourself. Do you ever depend on others but then blame them when they don't come through? Relying on other people can help us feel like we are needed, but when we attack them with negative energy, we hurt ourselves in the interactions.

Avoiding the real issues will never allow you to be free of worry. Instead of blaming others or trying to solve problems by dancing around the issues that concern you, be straightforward and address them head on.

• • •

I do not dance around the issues in my life. I am honest with others and myself, and when an issue arises, I address it openly. Other people respect me because I am honest with them. When I express my truth, I stand in integrity as I honor myself and my relationship with others.

• • •

What relationship in my life needs more honesty?

I AM PATIENT WITH MYSELF.

Forgive yourself. Please don't be so hard on yourself. You are doing the best you can. When you are kind to yourself, you will feel more productive and successful. Instead of condemning yourself, be patient. The journey to your heart is a sacred adventure, one that takes time. It is a process of learning about yourself through the journey of life.

• • •

I am learning and growing everyday. I am patient with myself as I try new things. I am also kind to myself through the process of healing. On the journey of reaching my goals, I create a timeline that aligns with my highest good. Even when things don't happen when I want them too, I am patient and I trust divine timing and myself.

• • •

Where should I be more patient with myself?

I GIVE UP CONTROL.

You may want to control certain outcomes in your life, and even people. It is natural for humans to want security and when we control our environment, we create a false sense of security. Trying to maintain balance through controlling anything is never a way to achieve what you want. By giving up control and allowing others to support you and show up for you, you will feel more loved. Trusting the universe is a large part of releasing the reins on your life. Hand over your worriers and concerns to the universe and you will be guided to love.

• • •

I release my need to control my life and those in it. I turn my worries over to the universe and know I am safe and secure. I release my need for approval of others and I accept them as they are. I give up control of trying to know or figure out how things are supposed to work out instead; I navigate my own life adventure with grace and ease.

• • •

Where can I give up control in my life?

I STAY ON PROJECTS UNTIL I SEE A SUCCESSFUL CONCLUSION.

Don't give up on your dreams or projects. Today is a reminder that all things take time and will manifest at their own pace. Instead of rushing a project or quitting before it is complete, pull yourself into the journey of the project and find the fun. Great joy can be found in the creation process. Instead of focusing so much on the end result, how can you be more in the process?

• • •

I don't give up on projects. I am accountable for my life and I successfully see things through until the end. When I align my heart and head, I am unstoppable. Everything I touch is golden, like the Midas Touch. My projects are full of love and I complete them with joy.

• • •

What details of a project or goal do I need to focus more on?

I GIVE OTHERS THE BENEFIT OF THE DOUBT.

You have a choice. You can trust people the first time you meet them, or you can distrust them until they earn it. When you give people the benefit of the doubt, you see the good and allow them to show you their true colors. There is no need to judge others for their actions or suspect they are being dishonest. Give them the benefit of the doubt and watch how your communication will deepen.

• • •

I see the good in others. I give them the benefit of the doubt and I leave my own issues out of situations. I approach each relationship nonjudgmentally and with an open mind. I believe in the good of others and trust their character.

• • •

Who can I forgive and give the benefit of the doubt?

I AM NOT POWERLESS.

You are not powerless. The entrapment you feel is not based on real information. Fear has created a shadow over your life and is making you feel stuck. You can always do something. Retreat into your heart and let your inner voice give you guidance. You will soon know the next right step for you to make as you move forward.

You are never alone. A large support system is waiting to help you. Just ask for guidance and you will receive the support you need.

• • •

I am not powerless. I make choices from a loving place and I connect to my heart for guidance. I have a choice and I embrace love. My energy is full of love and I release all fears. I am not trapped. I can move forward and free myself from this pain.

• • •

Where do I feel powerless and what can I do to move forward?

MY SELF-RESPECT AND DIGNITY ARE MY TOP PRIORITY.

You must not stay in any relationship or situation that makes you feel less than the amazing person you are. Today is a gentle reminder you should be your own top priority. Look at all of your relationships and see where you are sacrificing yourself to make another person happy. Focus on your own happiness, by making yourself a priority.

• • •

I am in the best relationship of my life, one with myself. I meet my needs with compassion and joy and I am my top priority. I respect myself by removing all negative relationships and people from my life. I am kind, loving and compassionate to myself and my desires manifest with dignity.

• • •

In what ways can I make myself my top priority?

I CAN LAUGH AT MYSELF.

Life can be stressful. It may feel as though you are stuck in a series of obstacles to overcome. Pay attention to your energy. Are you stuck in the mundane, worrying about every situation or wrongdoing? Maybe you are stressing about the controllable and uncontrollable outcomes of life. When you put your happiness in external situations, you may fail to see the humor and raw honesty of life.

There is no need to take yourself so seriously. Finding the humor in seemingly troubling situations can bring more joy into your life. When you can lighten up and laugh at yourself, you will feel truly free. Don't take yourself so seriously. A smile can transform any difficult situation.

• • •

I am easy-going and carefree. I can laugh at myself and be free to look at situations in a lighthearted manner. Life is a joy and a fun journey. I laugh and can see the humor in all situations. I don't take myself too seriously.

• • •

How can I lighten up a little more?

I EAT MY FOOD GUILT-FREE.

Food is love. It is a form of nourishment and source of energy for sustainability. However, you may feel guilty when you want certain types of food. It is common to feel as though you shouldn't want that chocolate cake or those french fries, especially if you want to be healthy. Society puts a lot of pressure on you to eat specific foods. Naturally, if you enjoy certain foods that are not in the category of what is considered healthy, you feel guilty. But imagine if there were no right and wrong and everything you ate was considered good for you.

For today, pretend everything you put in your mouth is healthy. When you truly enjoy your food and practice conscious eating, this is possible. There is no need to resist or fight food. You can love yourself and your body by eating foods guilt-free.

• • •

I take the pressure off of myself by eating all my food with love. I savor each bite and appreciate the flavors. Being present with my food has released the burden of guilt so I can be free to be true to me. I eat what I want and listen to my body as guidance for when I am full. I am healthy, vibrant and at my ideal body weight. I eat all food guilt-free.

• • •

What food do I feel guilty eating?
How can I transform this guilt into love?

I AM GENEROUS WITH MY TIME AND ENERGY. I SUPPORT THOSE I LOVE.

You may feel burdened by your own life stress and demands, but this is a perfect time to reach out and support others. When you feel stuck or stale in your own life, this is usually an indication of something missing. You have a natural desire to help others and when you are generous with yourself by sharing your time, energy, resources and love, you help yourself. You will feel more balanced and be more focused and happy.

• • •

I give without expecting anything in return. I am generous with my own resources by sharing my time, money, energy and love with those around me. I support those I love by sharing my own abundance. The universe is abundant and ever-supplying for my needs. I give unto others so I can be true to myself.

• • •

What friend can I support by giving my time?

MY SELF-SABOTAGING HABITS HAVE A MESSAGE FOR ME. I LISTEN TO THE GUIDANCE.

You don't need to feel guilty or put yourself through pain. If you have addictions or habits you feel guilty about, don't resist them. Instead, go into them and ask why they are there. When you can listen to your own body's wisdom, you will see the reason for self-sabotage and addictions. You may be using these habits as a crutch to avoid facing a painful issue in your life. Awareness is the key to transformation.

• • •

I allow myself to heal through my awareness. I am in tune with my body's needs and my true desires. I look deeply into my habits with love and compassion. Everything I need to heal is right here inside of me.

I send white light to my body's pain and flood my being with love. I am peaceful and connected to my body's wisdom. I listen to the guidance of my habits and transform them with love.

• • •

What compassionate message does my self-sabotaging habit have for me?

THE LITTLE THINGS I DO MAKE A BIG DIFFERENCE.

You may feel like you are not making a big enough difference in your life. The quality of your life is not determined by how many people you help or heal or how big of a difference you make. It is determined by how many little things you do with great love.

Look at everyday little things, such as opening a door for a stranger, buying coffee for a friend or helping a homeless person by giving money or food. These small acts of kindness can make a giant impact that will resonate forever. The little acts of kindness are more important than waiting for an opportunity to do some big, grandiose gesture. Put more attention to the mini-moments that bring opportunity for support and love.

• • •

I put extreme care into all I do. I make an impact in everyone's life because I am focused on the power of the present moment. I practice being present and I help and support those in need. My desire to help is my greatest asset to happiness. When I do small things with great love, I am living my purpose.

• • •

What little act of kindness can I do today?

I START EACH DAY WITH A GRATEFUL HEART.

Kristine Carlson says how you start your day is how you live your day. Think about how you woke up this morning. Were you frantic, focused on getting into the day and in a hurry? Or did you take a deep breath, soak in the new day's life and stretch, say a pray or maybe a meditation and give thanks?

When you wake up with a grateful heart, your entire day unfolds more smoothly. Try it out. When you wake up, before you even open your eyes, give thanks. Declare to the universe, God, your higher power, your angels, your dog, the air, or your significant other what you are thankful for.

• • •

I am thankful for another day to be alive. I am thankful for my health and my happiness. I love my bed and my home and I feel safe and secure. I am grateful for the beautiful world we live in. I can't wait to live my day. I am excited for life and eager to see how my day unfolds. I release the need to control anything. Instead, I am having fun along my journey of life.

• • •

How can I cultivate a morning gratitude practice?

I AM CONNECTED TO MY WORK.

The work you do is connected to your life plan. You have a unique set of skills, talents and strengths that are core to who you are. When you can utilize these key values in your work, you will be rewarded financially as well as spiritually. Doing what you love for a living is possible, but identify what you care about first.

Do you love helping people? Do you see yourself as a leader or are you more comfortable following? (A great resource to help you understand your own strengths is *Strength Finder 2.0,* by Tom Rath.) Knowing your strengths and living by your values are the keys to a happy life.

• • •

I do what I love everyday. My work does not feel like work because I am so connected to what I do, using my personal strengths, values and talents. I am a unique individual expressing my true self through my chosen work field. I am connected to the work I do because I know it is helping the greater good. I am of service to the world and I am rewarded financially.

• • •

How can I find more passion for my current job?

I AM RESPONSIBLE FOR CHANGING MY BEHAVIOR UNTIL I GET WHAT I WANT.

If you are frustrated with the outcome of recent actions, try again. Your life is an expansive unfolding of lots of experiments. Some experiments work, others do not. Part of living a rich, fulfilling life is being fully present in your journey. This means you are responsible for all you see. If you don't like the results, then change your behavior until you get what you want. Approach your life as an experiment. To get the results you want, keep changing your behavior until you find what works.

• • •

I am responsible for my experience of life. I choose to focus on the results I want to see, instead of dwelling on what didn't work in the past. I approach my life with open arms, and I behave my way to success.

• • •

What behavior can I shift to try to get new results?

I STOP WORRYING ABOUT DEBT.

Having debt is one thing. Worrying about it is a completely different situation. You may have financial debt and this can cause a strain on your relationships and your self-worth. Focusing on the debt causes tremendous pain and it can actually prevent you from getting out of debt.

When you focus on the problem, the problem persists. Instead, focus on a solution. Take action steps to consolidate your loans and debt and make a plan to pay it off each month. Focusing on the solution of any problem will get you faster results than dwelling on the problem.

• • •

There is no need to worry about financial debt. I am comfortable with myself and I know the universe is abundant. I release my lack mentality and allow money to flow to me. I actively work to pay off my debt by focusing on a solution. I take all my attention off of what is not working so I can focus on what is. A payment plan I am part of helps me control my finances and release the worry.

• • •

What date will I be debt-free by?
(Set a date to help empower yourself.)

I FORGIVE EX-LOVERS.

Holding on to past relationships after they expire is part of healing a broken heart. When you love someone, you will never truly get over them, for love is love and it can never die. The form of the love changes and you may be in a position where you are no longer with the person you once loved. Maybe they have moved on or you have, but there is still residue of emotional pain. When you hold onto emotions and replay negative aspects of the relationship, you put yourself in a holding pattern of anger. Releasing that anger and letting go of regret will help you welcome in a new start.

Forgiving your ex-lovers doesn't mean saying what happened is okay. It just means you have accepted the situation and can now see the big picture. When you forgive, it is not about the other person. It is about you opening up your future because you have finally forgiven your past.

• • •

Through this meditation mantra, bring up a person from your past who you would like to forgive:

I forgive you. You and I were part of a sacred plan that both of our souls signed on for. You taught me valuable lessons about life and myself. I never meant to hurt you and the pain I feel is because you will always have a place in my heart. I forgive you. I wish you well. I release this energetic hold and trust happiness and health is on its way to you. Thank you for being in my life and helping me become more of who I really am. I am forever grateful for our time together. You will have a place in my heart forever.

• • •

Who can I forgive?

WHEN I HELP OTHERS,
I HELP MYSELF.

Perhaps recent events have caused you to worry about the state of the world and its affairs. You may feel powerless and hopeless. When you are overwhelmed with worry, it makes it difficult to feel happiness. You may feel like you don't matter and nothing you do will really help. Even one small act of kindness can help thousands of people.

If you feel as if something is missing in your life, it could be your connection to others. You may be trying to find happiness in activities and outside circumstances, but it still eludes you. When you chase happiness, it can never reach you. Instead focus on how you can help others. Just donating time, money or energy to a cause you care about will help you feel more grounded. If you are sad and consumed with worry, volunteer and help another person or charity. You can adopt a pet or find ways to help others. This has a profound impact on you increasing your own happiness. When you help others, you help yourself.

• • •

True happiness comes when my words and actions help others. I enjoy giving my time, energy and resources to help those in need. I know my problems may feel overwhelming, but when I get out of my own way and help other people, I end up helping myself. There is a power in me supporting another person. It helps me become less focused on my own pain and put things into perspective. When I help others, I help myself.

• • •

What friend or family member can I help?

I CAN LOOK IN THE MIRROR AND LOVE MYSELF UNCONDITIONALLY.

There are times when you may get down on yourself and dislike who you see in the mirror. But you are much too hard on yourself. You are a beautiful being of light and love. Looking in the mirror and accepting yourself is part of living a peaceful life. When you are at peace with who you are, you become a beacon of light for others.

The truth is you judge yourself, but no one is judging you because they are busy judging themselves. The flaws you think people see are never noticed nor examined. You are your own worst critic. Recognize the shame you feel is all internal. Send love to yourself and practice acceptance.

You are perfect as you are. If you have a difficult time liking who you see in the mirror, practice will help make you feel perfect. Spend at least three minutes every day just staring into your eyes in the mirror. Send yourself loving thoughts and compliment yourself. This will help you befriend yourself.

• • •

I practice self-love by being kind to myself. I accept the person I am today and I can look in the mirror and send myself love. I am living my truth, which is a beacon of light and joy. I connect with my true self and love who I am unconditionally.

• • •

Go to the mirror and look at yourself for three
minutes. Send yourself love and light.
What compliments can I give myself?

I DON'T FEEL GUILTY
FOR WEIGHT GAIN.

Gaining weight is part of life. Whether you are recovering from a breakup, sickness or disease, recently had a baby or you love to eat, weight gain is not something to look at as bad. It does not make you flawed or unworthy. Society puts enormous pressure on people to be and stay thin. This creates a false illusion that if you gain weight, you are broken.

The truth is weight is just a reflection of life. Some years, you may weigh more than others. Instead of mentally berating yourself for gaining weight, send your entire body – including the extra pounds – love. When you approach your body with kindness, it will take off the pressure of guilt. This will help you step into a healing place to accept and return to your true body weight best for you.

• • •

For today, I am exactly where I need to be. The weight on the scale does not define me or determine my place in this world. I am much too hard on myself. I choose to release all guilt and blame and accept myself fully. I know others don't judge me the way I judge myself. I release this burden for good.

• • •

What can I do today that I couldn't do when I was thinner?
(It's not about the weight. Celebrate who you are today.)

I SHOW THE WORLD MY WEIRD, CRAZY, BEAUTIFUL SELF.

Don't be afraid to show the world who you are. You may fear people won't understand you or you won't fit in. But the truth is the more honest you are with yourself about who you are, the more the world can accept you.

Challenge yourself to show the quirks and habits you hide. Be more honest with yourself by embracing your true self, the crazy in you. Your crazy is part of what others need to see so they don't feel so alone. Stop hiding yourself from the world and show off your beautiful, crazy, weird self.

• • •

Nothing is standing in my way. I show up for myself by showing the world who I am. I embrace my quirky, weird and funny characteristics. I don't have any habits I keep secret. I show people who I really am. When I do this, I get the honest reflection back. Because I am in love with myself and showing the world my true self, the world accepts and honors me as I am.

• • •

What secretive habit can I share with others?

I INSPIRE OTHERS WITH MY OWN BIGNESS.

You have greatness inside you bigger than your body. All of your hopes and dreams are tucked deep in your soul. You are unlike anyone else in the world, which means you can inspire others by you being you.

You may not feel confident or comfortable showing others your dreams or certain aspects of your personality, but this lack of confidence is usually tied to past experiences where shame was at play. Forgive your past and those who hurt you.

When you see how wonderful you are, you will release the confines of worry. Look at how much you have been able to accomplish in your life. Look at proof of your greatness in action. You are like a super human that makes things happen. You have defied the odds and overcome turbulent times. Start singing the praise of your greatness. Take more risks because your greatness will support it.

• • •

I am over being down on myself. I am sick of selling myself short. Today is a new beginning. I stand tall, confident and proud of who I am. I choose to show the world my true self and all of my wonder. I am full of love and shining brightly from passion and purpose. I am great. I celebrate my greatness.

• • •

Who inspires me with their own greatness?
Which of those qualities is reflected me?

I LIVE MY VALUES.

You have a power system ingrained in your soul. These are your personal values, the ones unique to you. No one else in the world has the same internal value system as you. When you identify and live your values, you will feel internal happiness. The universe will reward you for being true to yourself and your relationships, career and life will flourish.

To identify your values, think about your childhood and what was most important to you. Helping others, expressing yourself creatively, moving your body with physical activity, such as dance, etc. Your childhood is your source of inspiration because it represents you at your purest form. Identify and live your values for a happy approach to life.

• • •

I am in love with my life. I live my values and show up with integrity in all my interactions. My values are a reflection of my souls deepest desires. When I live from my heart, my values are effortless and in front focus. My life is balanced and I am happy because I set an example of what's possible. When I live my life by my own values, I guide others to do the same.

• • •

What are my values?

I STAY HOPEFUL AND OPTIMISTIC IN DIFFICULT SITUATIONS.

Hope is your flashlight guiding you into happiness. When you are trapped by difficult situations, hope will guide you home. You always have what it takes to proceed and move through challenging times. It may feel as though there is no way out, but turning to hope will help you. You can focus on the positive aspects instead of the pain. Finding hope will help you overcome the troubling time.

When you feel a rush of excitement and worry-free energy, this is a signal you are grasping hope. Hope and optimism will be your compass, guiding you back to the light. Where there is love, there is always hope. Turn your fears over to the universe and reach for love.

• • •

I am hopeful in all areas of my life. I reach for good-feeling vibrations. I know difficult situations often bring great understanding of self-awareness and I dive into my situations with attention on healing. I look for the good and see the positive aspects of each situation. I am aligned with my truth, which is love. I turn my fears over to the universe, love will guide me home.

• • •

What can I be more optimistic about?

I SEE EVERYONE AS AN EQUAL.

Your relationships are the greatest opportunity for growth and understanding. Which means the people in your life who cause the most emotional stress also offer the greatest opportunity for self-expansion. If someone in your life is causing you frustration, take a step back and see him or her as an equal. Having empathy for others will help expand your relationships.

If you are connected to an outcome or hoping another person will do what you want them to do, release this need for control. Everyone has their own set of struggles, beliefs and situations they are going through. When you can release all judgment and let others be who they are, not who you think they should be, you will feel free.

• • •

I do not play favorites or look at others with a discerning eye. I am committed to growing and show up with non-judgmental energy. I see everyone as the same. We are all working through life together, navigating our own struggles. There is no need for me to reflect my pain on others nor do I take on theirs. Instead I send love to everyone and accept that we are all equal.

• • •

Who do I need to see as equal?

I ACCEPT THAT GOOD IS GOOD ENOUGH.

Stop working so hard trying to be perfect. Perfection is a silent killer that eats away your time, money and energy. When you focus on the perfect outcome, you miss out on being in the process.

Accepting that enough is enough and sometimes good is good enough is the key to freedom and happiness. Give yourself permission to release the control and turn inward for self-acceptance. When you accept yourself, the actions and projects you create will always be good enough.

• • •

I stop trying so hard to make sure everything is perfect. There is no need for me to work so hard to be perfect. The perfection is in the moment, and accepting that good is more than good enough is my real freedom. I let go of all the time I spend trying to make it perfect and see others do not examine things the way I do. I am no longer hard on myself. I let go of control and celebrate the situation as it is.

• • •

What situation can I stop trying to improve
and accept that it is good enough?

I AM COMFORTABLE SAYING THANK YOU.

It's nice to hear thank you. Other people in your life care deeply about you and want nothing but your happiness and health. When they reach out to do kind things for you, remember to say thank you. You may be thankful for things in your life and you may feel it, but today is a gentle reminder to cultivate the practice of verbalizing your thanks.

Giving thanks can be in the form of gifts, attention, time, money and energy, but often the simplest of thank yours is a verbal *I appreciate you*. Thank you is a beautiful expansion of your human spirit. Being comfortable saying thank you helps those around you feel connected to you. You will see more love and appreciation when you can verbally share your gratitude.

• • •

I wake up with a grateful heart and feel gratitude for all that is good. I love to show my appreciation for everything in my life by saying thank you. When I share my gratitude, others feel appreciated and respected. It is important for me to show what I am thinking. Appreciating others and their efforts is part of my own well-being. I give thanks openly and freely. When people pay me a compliment, I accept it with grace. I can accept compliments and I give them freely. I am grateful for all in my life.

• • •

Who has always been there for me that I
can verbally say thank you to?

I SET HIGH EXPECTATIONS.

Raising your standards is part of growing into your best self. When you start to show up for yourself and cultivating a practice of happiness, you will naturally raise your expectations. Setting high expectations is an opportunity for you to prove your own worth.

You don't need to prove or show others anything. But by increasing your own standards, you show yourself how valuable you are. All areas of your life can have standards, your health, your relationships, your financial well-being and your career. Look at every aspect of your life and ask yourself where you can set higher expectations.

• • •

I matter. My life is reflection of my goals manifested into action. I set high expectations for myself because it helps push me out of my comfort zone and reach new heights. By setting higher standards, I overcome new challenges and live a more full life. I do not settle in any area of my life. I am aligned with my best self and I set high expectations.

• • •

Where can I set higher expectations?

I AM RESILIENT.

Bouncing back from life's difficult situations is what you are a master at. It may feel like the situation you are currently in will never end, but this is a reminder how resilient you are. You can overcome anything and will with grace and power. Align inward with your inner light and focus on the loving presence around you.

During difficult times it's easy to feel like you are alone, but there is plenty of support around you and willing to help. Be open to guidance and be open to receiving help. Your resilience is an asset that will carry you forward.

• • •

I am so much stronger than I give myself credit for. I am an overcomer, and achiever, a doer and a fighter. I can rise above any situation with grace and power. I am resilient. When I am in difficult situations I reach out to the support around me. I let help in and allow those around me to help.

I overcome life's challenging moments because I am capable, willing and strong. Every situation I experience is part of my greater understanding of life. I navigate through the difficult times with a strong determination and will to succeed. I can do this. I am an achiever. I am resilient.

• • •

What have I bounced back from?

Setbacks do not define me;
they nudge me into a
new awareness.

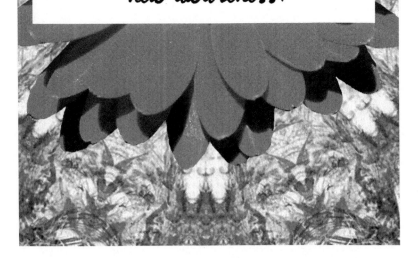

SETBACKS DO NOT DEFINE ME. THEY NUDGE ME INTO A NEW AWARENESS.

Setbacks in your life are not indications of you being off track. They are opportunities for more self-awareness and growth. The situation that feels the most difficult to navigate is often in your life as a teacher. Each situation that feels like a setback is actually realignment.

If you were to be honest with yourself, you can examine the outcome and see it is putting you on a path for your highest good. When you go into each situation, ask yourself how it plays into your big picture. You will feel more grounded. The experience in your life will no longer feel chaotic or random.

• • •

I am peaceful. I am not attached to the outcome of situations in my life. I feel connected to my purposes and see how everything works together. The recent setbacks in my life are actually opportunities for me to realign with my values and true worth. When I am honest with myself, I see there is no such thing as a setback. I am always being nudged into a new awareness of self. I am connected to my life and I focus forward with love.

• • •

What current situation feels like a setback but could actually be putting me back on track?

I REWARD MYSELF WITH SIMPLE LUXURIES.

If you feel guilty for treating yourself, you are not alone. Most people want to make sure everyone else is cared for and then its time to care for themselves. For a balanced, happy and peaceful life, reverse this approach. Instead of waiting for others to be happy before you can, put yourself first. One simple way to do this is to reward yourself with simple pleasures.

Little luxuries, like a chocolate bar or a bouquet of flowers, buying a nice outfit or candles for your bath, are all part of treating yourself well. Treating yourself to small special treats makes the journey more enjoyable. It helps you reconnect with yourself and feel more balanced.

• • •

I treat myself to little gifts that bring my joy. I enjoy the process of investing in myself for it reminds me I am loved. I care about my wellness and I show up for myself daily. My enjoying the simple luxuries reminds me I make a difference in the world. When I take care of myself, I am take care of others.

• • •

What can I treat myself to today?

I LEAVE ALL UNHEALTHY SITUATIONS.

You most likely have been enduring a difficult situation for too long. The situation may be toxic and affecting your ability to be happy. You may have a hard time letting go because you have invested a lot of time, energy, and maybe even money, but ignoring the reality is hurting your health.

The experience you went through is the reward. The true benefit for your soul's growth will be revealed to you when you leave the unhealthy situation. Instead of looking at it as wasted energy and time, leave the unhealthy situation and free yourself.

You can walk away without hesitation or guilt. Ask the universe and friends for support that the parting is harmonious and for your highest good. But you know in your heart it is time.

• • •

I leave all unhealthy situations and walk away with confidence and peace in my heart. I am doing the right thing and all is in right order. There is nothing here for me. It is time to leave.

I release my need to know the reason this situation was part of my life, for in time this information will be revealed to me. I let go of everything unhealthy for me. I choose love and healthy opportunities can now come my way.

• • •

What unhealthy relationship will I let go of?

MY INNER VOICE IS TRUSTWORTHY.

You may be confused or feel uncertain. Today is a verification your inner voice is always speaking to you. You can trust the voice, for it will never lead you astray. Your heart speaks to you through your feelings, thoughts and ideas, and you are hearing it accurately.

Pay attention to how you feel in each situation and trust your instincts. It is safe to move forward with changes in your life. Your inner voice is your guide, helping you navigate the transition.

• • •

The feelings I feel are accurate and real. My inner voice is always talking to me. I trust the guidance and listen to it with an open heart and non-judgmental awareness. I am secure in myself and connected to my heart's desires. I trust the voice within. It is my truth.

• • •

What is my inner voice telling me and how can I trust it more?

IT IS ALREADY DONE.

You will be pleased with the outcome. The universe is working on your behalf to solve the problem. The universe is working on a plan beyond your scope of human understanding. You may not see evidence of things working out, but trust that the universe has solved your troubling situations.

Everything has already worked out. There is no need to carry the burden that things won't fall into place. Trust that the universe has already taken care of your situation and carry forward with the confidence you will get what you need.

• • •

I am excited about the opportunities in my future. Everything is falling into place. Nothing is out of order. The universe has created a master plan and my desires are in motion. Everything I need is on its way to me. It is already done. There is nothing to worry about.

• • •

In what situation can I hand my worries over to the universe and trust they will be taken care of?

I DETACH FROM ALL TROUBLING SITUATIONS AND SURROUND THEM WITH LOVE.

You may be in a situation causing you pain. You are so embodied in the experience, you can no longer see it objectively. Look carefully at the big picture and surround yourself with love. Take the emotion out of the situation and see it is not about you. You can take the attachment out by depersonalizing the situation and objectively observing the outcome.

There is no need to take offense to others' behaviors. The situation is clouded with fear and judgment. When you give yourself permission to take time away and detach, you will see it more clearly. The objective point of view will help you through this situation.

• • •

I refrain from judgment or seeing painful situations with fear. I detach myself from the experience and allow love to come in. Instead of looking at what others are doing wrong, I send them love and light for healing. When I detach from the situation, I am at peace and the situations can heal.

• • •

What situation can I remove myself from?

I AM ALWAYS ON THE EDGE OF MY POTENTIAL.

The most successful and fulfilled people in the world have one thing in common. They push themselves to the edge of their potential. You have unlimited potential inside of you. Listen to your heart. It will show you the way forward to reach your full purpose. Now is a great time to set goals and work toward them. With actionable goals, you set yourself up for success by having a road map to follow. Your potential is in the goals and dreams you hold in your heart. By following your heart and doing what you love, your anxieties will fade.

• • •

I am living my dream life. I am always aligned with my truth, which is an expression of love. I choose to see my life as a creative adventure, one in which I explore my full potential. I live on the edge of my own creativity and push forward into new possibilities.

• • •

What new possibilities can I create for myself?

OPPORTUNITIES FLY AT ME.

Position yourself to believe opportunities are everywhere. You will get results based on your expectations. When you expect good things to happen, you will see evidence in the making. Instead of focusing on problems, become solution-focused and see the opportunities around you. There is always something you can do, another possibility to try. Go for what you want and seek out support to help you get what you want. The universe is supporting you and will deliver what you desire.

• • •

I hold faith that everything is in perfect order. Opportunities are everywhere and I am abundant ands secure. My life is a reflection of my positive thoughts and I see the results of my actions. I am living my dream life with new opportunities on the horizon. I celebrate all I am becoming and seek out new opportunities as they come.

• • •

What opportunities can I embrace?

I AM A WHY NOT PERSON.

There are two types of people in the world. The *why not* people and the *why bother*. When it comes to making your dreams come true, embrace the *why not* attitude. If you say *why bother,* then you sell yourself short. There will be many opportunities for you to give up on your dream. Don't. Fear and self-doubt will try to sabotage your efforts. Your mission is to keep moving forward with a can-do attitude. Embrace the *why not* and you will reach your goal.

• • •

I do not allow my fears to derail me. When I get inspiration, I act on it with a nothing is impossible attitude. Instead of turning to why bother, I embrace the idea anything is possible. When I put my mind to it, I can accomplish anything. There is no limitations accept those I put on myself.

• • •

What dream can I go for?

I GO FOR WHAT I WANT, NOT JUST WHAT I THINK IS POSSIBLE.

Pay attention to your thoughts. If you're settling into what you think is possible, you may be selling yourself short. You might be basing your potential off of failed opportunities or mistakes from your past. When you think about reaching your goals, do you go for what you want or settle for what you assume is possible? Make sure you are reaching for the stars and giving yourself permission to dream big.

The universe will support you in reaching your goals, but setting a clear intention is essential. Let the dreams that live inside your heart lead the way.

• • •

I go for what I want in life and I get it. I dream big and action out my goals. I don't settle nor do I sink into self-sabotage or doubt. I go for what I want, not just what is possible. I know when inspiration comes, it is my mission to act on it. The dreams that come to me are part of my sacred contract. I go for what I want and live my dreams daily.

• • •

Where can I dream bigger and actually go for what I want, instead of settling for what I think I can get?

MY LIFE IS AN EXPERIMENT. I EMBRACE THE EXPLORATION.

Dive into your life as if it was a giant exploration and epic journey. Life should be approached as an experiment. You get to create, try and retry different experiments. When you go for what you want and it doesn't work out the way you hoped, it's not a failure or a mistake. It is part of the deep dive and rich exploration.

Embrace your life as if it were a game of trial and error. You get to try things and see what works and what doesn't. When you look at your life as an experiment, you will be less burdened by external situations.

• • •

I live my life fully by setting intentions and exploring new ways of being. I connect with my divine truth, which shows me the next action step to take. I explore my life as if it were a creative adventure. I am on an epic journey to my heart. I enjoy trying new things and seeing new outcomes.

• • •

What experiment am I currently trying?

I SMILE AT STRANGERS.

The simple act of smiling can make you feel better. When you smile, the feel-good neurotransmitter dopamine is released. This helps you feel more relaxed and happy. Smiling is a form of kindness. Not only does it help you feel better, but it makes you more approachable.

Smiling at other people builds a connection and helps establish rapport. Step out of your comfort zone by making eye contact and smiling at strangers. You may surprise yourself with a new connection. Strangers are just friends you have yet to meet and a smile can bridge that gap.

• • •

I smile confidently and with great love. I look at others and welcome them into my life. I am connected to my best self, who is happy, healthy and open to meeting others. When I smile at strangers, they feel warm and respected. I am happy to share smiles with those I love. We are all connected and a smile brings us closer.

• • •

How has my smile helped me get close to others?

ALL NEW THINGS REQUIRE DISCOMFORT.

When you embark on a self-improvement path you may grow uncomfortable. New habits create new results, but this produces a new way of being. When you desire something, you have to become the person who can receive that desire. This is why there is a universal buffer between what you want, and where you currently stand.

You have to learn, grow change and become more of the person you truly want to be. This is a natural part of life, but one that will require you to be uncomfortable. All new stages of your life require discomfort. Learning how to be comfortable when you are uncomfortable is the key to success.

• • •

I am open to change. I am growing more into the person I want to become. I am comfortable with the uncomfortable aspect of growth. I know that all greatness requires a transition period, I navigate mine gracefully. I grow with dedication and commitment to becoming more of who I really am.

• • •

What recent change has caused me to be uncomfortable?

I SET FUN AND RECREATION GOALS.

You may feel the need for more balance in your life. If you are stressed out or overwhelmed with particular demands, it is essential to carve out more you time. One successful strategy is to actually schedule fun time into your schedule. Playtime is essential for your happiness and productivity, but setting goals in this arena will boost your happiness ten fold.

Create a big picture view of your life, and think about what is most important to you when it comes to having more fun and recreation in your life. Have you always wanted to explore a near by city, or try a new hobby? Set fun goals for yourself and watch yourself become more balanced.

• • •

I set goals that are fun and actionable. I create time for me and carve out space to play. When I add more play into my life I am connected to my true self and I am balanced.

• • •

What fun goal can I set for myself?

NATURE IS MY SANCTUARY.

If you are feeling frustrated, overwhelmed, stressed or anger, return to your natural state, one that is in harmony with the world. Going into nature will help calm your body and mind. Nature has no anger. It is patient and nature is kind. There is a natural flow and understanding to all things in nature.

The tree does not yell at itself, hurry up and grow, it takes its time, and patience is its virtue. The same goes for grass that grows toward the sunlight. It reaches for fresh air. Nature can be your greatest teacher to help you return to self and learn valuable life lessons.

• • •

When I become anxious I return to my true self, which is one in harmony with the world. I am balanced because I seek sanctuary in nature. Being in nature helps me heal my worries and return to happiness.

• • •

How can I bring more nature into my life?

I AM A HEALER.

You have a great healing capacity inside of you. You may feel rundown or troubled by sickness in yourself or others, but this does not need to stop you from shining your authentic light. Focus on your healing capabilities with love and compassion. You may be sensitive to the needs of those closest to you. You can help them by being there for them. Often, behind the smiles there is pain. You can become the restorer of happiness by holding space for others.

You don't need to judge or try to fix anyone, just be with them. You are a vessel of light and love, and by sharing this with others you heal yourself and the world. Too often, you become fixated on your own situations. Today is a reminder you can encourage the discouraged. Don't wait for a miracle. Become the miracle.

• • •

I can heal the world. I lift up those who are down with my encouragement and love. I am compassionate in all of my endeavors and interactions. I see light where there is darkness. I see hope where there is hopelessness. I see love in the face of fear. I am a healer and a light worker. I have the capacity to change the world by focusing on love.

• • •

How can I be there for those who are hurting?

ALL DISEASE AND DISCOMFORT ARE A MANIFESTATION OF A THOUGHT PATTERN IN MY MIND.

Your thoughts are an integral part of your expression of life. What you think, you become. When you feel out of alignment or not balanced, return to your thoughts and focus on holding positive energy. The disease in your body is a manifestation of thoughts from your previous path.

If you hold onto negative patterns, they will form into outward expressions. Release all fear-based thoughts and cleanse yourself regularly. You can clear yourself with white light and with the meditation below.

• • •

I create loving expressions of my truth. My body is in perfect health. Any dis-ease I experience is an opportunity for me to learn more about myself.

I choose healthy habits for my body and life. I move in a way that helps serve my greatest good. I focus on what is essential for me to move forward and I embody my sprit as I create healthy habits to help me move forward. I release all fear-based thoughts and attach myself to positive energy. I am free of physical pain and worry. I am centered in my truth.

• • •

Where can I be more true to myself and
align with positive intentions?

I REALIGN WITH MY DESIRES DAILY.

It is okay to refresh yourself and take steps to cultivate new habits. Today is about being more vulnerable with yourself. Look at your identity and who you are. Discern what is important to you. Certain relationships, things and situations in your life might be blocking you from reaching your goals. It is important for you to realign with your goals and do this daily.

You are always changing and growing. Becoming more of who you are is a process and with that comes new desires. Allow yourself to assess and recalibrate your goals to make sure you are aligned with your truth.

• • •

I am connected to my highest vibration and truth. When I focus forward, I leave no room for error because my heart is in the driver's seat of my life. I am aligned with my soul's purpose and true desires. I reevaluate often to ensure I am aligned with my highest good. All my desires are manifesting with love and I am comfortable in the process.

• • •

What desire do I need to revisit?

I CHOOSE MY WORDS WISELY.

Expressing yourself through language is a gift. The words you choose have a powerful impact on your overall outcome. When you choose words like "hate," you are sending out negative energy. What you resist will always persist. Make a conscious effort not to say words that shed evil energy. Find a better way to release anger. Your words are powerful expressions of your truth. Use your words wisely.

• • •

I choose my words with conscious focus and energy. I do not use unnecessary words to get my point across. All of my vocabulary is part of my essence and how I project myself into the world. I choose positive words that are uplifting and energetically light. I do not send hateful words out into the world. I reach out to my enemies with love and kindness. My words are my greatest expressions of self.

• • •

What words can I eliminate from my vocabulary?

I ACTIVELY LIVE MY HIGHEST AWARENESS.

You are always changing, growing, morphing into more of who you really are. You are not the same person you were when you woke up this morning, nor are you the same person as you were a year ago. Let yourself grow and change as you learn more and expand your consciousness. Holding onto old beliefs out of habit will not serve you. It is time to spread your wings and let yourself fly.

• • •

I am changing. I am growing. All my senses come to life as I morph into the new me that awaits. The universe is guiding me to new beginnings as I co-create with my highest good. I live from integrity and I live out my truth. I trust what I know and my new awareness leads me to happiness and true health.

• • •

What new beginning am I being guided to?

I DO NOT BUY INTO OTHER PEOPLE'S EVALUATIONS OF ME.

What people say to you or about you is not fact. You don't have to accept their evaluations. You can believe them or you can believe in yourself. The only thing that matters is how you see yourself. People will always have a point of view, but your only mission is to evaluate yourself based on love and compassion. You can never judge a person's life or understand what they are going through. Let others have their opinions but pay no attention to them.

• • •

I am happy to be me. I am comfortable with myself and pay no attention to what others say or think about me. When I am proud of myself and my accomplishments, I don't need the approval of others. I do not buy into other people evaluations of me. I only care about what I think about myself.

• • •

What hurtful thing did someone say about me that I can let go of?

EVERYONE IS ON HIS OR HER OWN JOURNEY.

Comparing yourself to others is hurting you. You either feel inferior or superior, but neither is the truth. Everyone is equal and you are your own unique person. You are a unique, wonderful spirit with beautiful gifts to give to the world. There is no one to compare yourself to because everyone is unique and on his or her own journey.

Everything in the physical world is part of transition and change. Comparing yourself to others is a waste of time because everything is always changing. Allow yourself to flow with changes and turn inward. Your true essence is your internal being. Your spirit is deeper and more real than any external body or change.

• • •

I love myself and other people unconditionally. I am unique and one of a kind. There is no other person who has ever been like me and I celebrate my oneness. There is nothing to compare, for I am on my own journey and I am true to myself.

• • •

Who do I keep comparing myself to? I release my need to be like others. I am my own unique self.

I EXPLORE MY FEARS SO I CAN RELEASE THEM FOR GOOD.

Fear is not bad. Fear is connected to your ego and your ego just wants to protect you. Instead of running from your fear, give it love. Fear is like a lonely child looking for attention. It will lash out to be heard and seen, but you don't have to let it control your life. If you look at your fear, the same way you would a young child, you will see it just needs attention. When you can see the truth behind your fear, it will no longer try to control you.

Resistance is outwardly experienced as fear. The amount of fear is equivalent to the degree of resistance. Which means the more fear you feel about a situation, the more certain you should be that the venture is important to the growth of your soul. If it meant nothing to you, you would feel no resistance. Resistance shows up to ask us to look deep into our heart to see what we care most about.

• • •

I am detached from the outcome. I am not afraid of my fear, for it is trying to guide me back to safety. I look at my fear and see what it is trying to tell me. The more fear I feel, the more attention that area of my life needs. Usually fear is an indicator of what I care about the most.

• • •

My fear is good. It is a compass into areas of growth. The more scared I am, the more sure I am that I have to go for it.

THE UNIVERSE IS TESTING ME.

Your life is a master plan of seasons inspired by your soul. You may have a dream you are working toward. The universe will test you. Areas of your life need more awareness and the universe will bring people, places and situations to you to help you overcome the challenges and learn the lessons.

You may ask the universe or pray for love. Trust you will always get what you ask for, but it might be in a different form. The universe may bring you unloving or unkind people. This is for you to practice what you desire. If you want to be more loving and committed to kindness, then practice it in the face of adversity. Everything is always changing, but your heart does not waver. What you desire is on its way to you, but you must be present to the universal lessons.

• • •

My power comes through my mind and my connection to my heart. The universe will test me, but I am always up for the challenge. I see opportunity in the expansive nature of being true to myself. I seek out what I desire and practice my values daily. I will attract what I want when I become what I want.

• • •

How is the universe testing me?

I ASK FOR FEEDBACK.

You may be in a current relationship or situation where you feel unsure of where it is going. If you are going along and feel stuck in the motions of life, look at your communication. Having a communication plan with others will help you feel more purposeful and connected.

In romantic relationships or work environments, opening yourself up to feedback will help you assess your overall plan. Be open to receiving information from others. Ask for feedback about your relationship, about your process and your own growth. Listening to others will help you revaluate and grow.

• • •

I am open to hearing from others and listening to their honest feedback. I want to improve my life and my communication with others. Feedback is essential for my growth and development. I take what works and leave what doesn't. Feedback is a communication tool that helps me connect with those I care about.

• • •

What relationship can I ask for feedback in?

I GET OUT OF THE BUT ZONE.

Look at a current situation that is causing you the most stress and see if you are making excuses. Are you blaming others or wondering why it hasn't happened yet? Maybe you are focusing on what you want but you keep falling into the but zone. The but zone is where you say, "I want to lose weight...*but* I am too tired to exercise." "I want to find a soul mate...*but* no one approaches me."

Where are you but-ing all over yourself? Focus back on your intentions and align with your desires. Leave the buts out of the equation and watch what you want come to you faster.

• • •

I refuse to make excuses for my circumstances. I am accountable and connected to my desires. What I experience is a direct reflection of what I have been thinking about. I know I don't have control over some things in my life, but I have control over my thoughts about my life. I can choose to focus on expansive opportunities and I stay out of the but zone.

• • •

What excuses will I kick to the curb?

CONTINUOUS EFFORT GIVES ME UNLIMITED POTENTIAL.

You might be feeling down and out. You have been focusing more attention on what isn't working than what is. When you are on a path of self-improvement, it is the mini-steps along the way that make the big path possible.

Stop focusing so much on what isn't working and put your energy into potential. No matter what, keep going. Do not give up. When the dream is in your heart, persistence is essential. It may take time to manifest, but when you hold the intention of why you want what you want, it will come true. Forget a timeline and just keep going.

• • •

I release my need to manifest the outcome and I trust divine timing. I am fully in the process of my life. I keep going and try new things. I know my dreams come true with continue focus and attention. I put forth all of my attention and live my unlimited potential.

• • •

What dream can I keep putting attention too?

I DON'T HAVE TO SEE THE WHOLE PATH. I TAKE ONE STEP AT A TIME.

Are you overwhelmed by the burden of the tasks in front of you? Your goals require action and when you get inspired, you should take steps forward. You don't have to know which action. There is no wrong action, as long as you are taking action forward.

You may be focusing too much on the end destination. Rewind your attention by focusing more on what you can do in this moment. One step at a time will give you the results your truly desire. Keep moving forward.

• • •

I trust my future and my plans are unfolding perfectly. I don't have to see the entire path. I just take one step at a time. Each step I take reveals the next best step forward. I am connected to my life's purpose by taking action and trusting the guidance I receive.

• • •

What one step can I take to help me get to my goal?

I AM CLEAR WITH MY INTENTIONS.

The clearer you are with what you desire, the easier your manifestation process will be. If you are going back and forth on what you want, the universe will waver as well. Get clear with your intentions and focus forward with energetic enthusiasm. When you hold the belief that your dreams are coming true, and you do not waiver, the manifestation will happen rapidly. Be clear with why you want what you want and do not back down on your dreams.

• • •

I do not let fear stop me. I focus on what I want and keep my attention focused on my desire. I am dedicated to my dreams and I align my actions to match my goals. Everything I do is focused on me receiving my goals. I am purposeful in my interactions and clear with my intentions.

• • •

What goal of mine needs more clarity?

MY FINANCIAL ABUNDANCE IS REFLECTED IN WHAT I SEE.

A limited belief or thought that may be holding you back is the belief there are not enough resources, time or money to go around. If you feel trapped by life's circumstances, look to the beliefs you have been carrying around about the situation. When you see others in abundance and prosperity, see it as a mirror of your own abundance and what is on its way to you. There is no need to feel a lack mentality or as though there is not enough for everyone. You are connected to your abundance when you focus on your worth.

• • •

My thoughts determine my own prosperity. I am worth what I think I am worth. I am grateful for what I have, for it increases my abundance and wealth. I recognize financial abundance in every experience and welcome it to me. I am abundant and secure.

• • •

What outward expression of wealth do I keep seeing?
How is this a reflection of my own desires?

I DETACH FROM SOCIAL VAMPIRES.

Look at all of your relationships and see who is bringing you down. Some people like to talk about their dramas, their insecurities and their fears. This energy can be draining and keep you from focusing on your best self. Disengage from negative people and detach from those relationships. When you do this, you will align with your own best self and feel more grounded.

Your positivity is important right now. Releasing friends who no longer serve you creates space to welcome in new, more optimistic friends. Surround yourself with positive and supportive people.

• • •

I let go of all demeaning relationships. I release my attachment to old friends who cause me frustration and stress. I surround myself with kind, loving and supportive people. Together we accomplish great things because my support system is solid and full of positive energy and light.

• • •

What relationship causes me the most emotional stress?
What steps can I take to release this person from my life?

I CREATE MY FUTURE BY ENVISIONING IT.

When you visualize what you want, you give the universe an opportunity to filter in resources to help you get it. You will only see enough to match your vision. So be careful to not limit yourself. Instead, expand your mind by removing limiting beliefs and negative thoughts. By visualizing your success, you will reach your goals faster. You have to believe it and see it before you can receive it.

• • •

I hold the vision of what I want. I do not spend time focusing on any negative thoughts or limiting beliefs. Every action I take keeps me on track to live my big picture plan. I create my ideal life by envisioning it every day.

• • •

What limiting belief is blocking me from creating my ideal future?

I create my future
by envisioning it.

I SEE THE REWARD IN TAKING RISKS.

All great outcomes involve great risk. Most risk involved is emotional, like in stepping out of your comfort zone and doing what you haven't done before. Assess your current comfort zone and see where you are playing it safe. Think about your core desire and what you want.

As you use this as your target to move forward, you will see the power of taking great risks. All risk has reward. You will gain valuable experiences and grow into who you are meant to be. Give yourself permission to go for it and try new experiments. To get the results you want, you will need to take greater risk.

• • •

I take risks with love and dedication to my greater good. I know what I want and I take steps to get there. All great challenges are overcome by taking risks. My reward is in the journey of life as I take more chances and grow. I invite new risk into my life for the reward will be gratifying.

• • •

What risk can I take to help reach my goal?

I ALLOW MYSELF TO JUST BE WHO I AM.

Love yourself in this very moment. As you are, no pretenses, no forced interactions. There is nothing for you to say and do. There is nothing for you to be. Accept who you are. If you believe you have to wait to accept yourself, when you lose weight or grow your hair out, or get the job or the relationship, or finally receive the financial support, you are keeping yourself on the outside looking in on your own life.

If you have ever lost the weight or had more money or were in a relationship, you know nothing would change. Self-acceptance comes from within. It does not come from the experiences outside of yourself. Drop your list of expectations and see how beautiful and awesome you really are.

• • •

I no longer resist accepting myself, for I am an expression of love. I enjoy showing the world who I really am. I am love. I drop my list of expectations and accept myself as I am. I allow myself to be who I really am.

• • •

What part of myself have I been unwilling to accept?

EVERYONE IS FAMILY.

You have your close family and you are surrounded by love. But all living beings are part of your family. Looking at strangers as outsiders hurts your ability to feel connected and appreciated.

Everyone you have ever met and come in contact with is part of an intricate web of universal souls connected to divine love. This unconditional love connects us all. When you refuse to forgive, you are hurting your family, therefore hurting yourself. When you only look at your families limitations, you fail to see the opportunities of compassion. Look at everyone as if they were part of your true family and you will feel more aligned with real love.

• • •

I choose my family. I have the perfect family for me to learn what I need to learn. My parents have given me valuable lessons in love, self-acceptance, forgiveness and loyalty. I let go of all limiting beliefs that separate me from others. Everyone in my life is part of a beautiful unconditional support system. We are all family. We are one.

• • •

What family member do I need to forgive?

I AM AWARE OF MY STORIES.

The limitations in your life are primarily caused by the stories in your mind. You have experiences from your past that have resulted in reactions, which create stories. The stories are illusions that separate you from the truth. Look deep into your heart to see the truth.

That person you think dislikes you is really just trying to make it through his or her own life. It has nothing to do with you. The comment your significant other made has nothing to do with you. The stories you create keep you playing small and prevent you from living to your full potential. Become aware of the message your stories are trying to tell you and release them for good.

• • •

I am honest with myself and see situations, as they are, not how I wish them to be. I do not lean on false fabrications of reality or on illusions. I turn to the truth and see things as they are. I take emotion out of situations so I can be connected to the truth and have an unbiased approach. I am aware of my stories and I transform them with love.

• • •

What story is preventing me from seeing my true greatness?

I DO NOT JUDGE MYSELF FOR FEELING MY FEELINGS.

Check in with yourself and see if you are judging yourself for feeling your feelings. So many people feel guilty for feeling angry because they can't feel happy. When you judge yourself for your emotions, you keep yourself in the vicious cycle of self-doubt and denial. Express your feelings as much as you can. Allow yourself to cry, scream in the car, or share your sadness with a significant other. Expressing your feelings means expressing your true nature. Don't deny yourself expressions of life.

• • •

I allow myself to feel my feelings. I do not judge myself or put limitations on how I feel. Each emotion is an energy that needs to be released. My feelings are all thoughts that vibrate in my body and I create my own healing by feeling my feelings. My honest expression of self is shared through my emotions.

• • •

How do I judge myself for certain feelings I feel?

I TAKE TIME TO GRIEVE.

The passing of a loved one or losing a person or pet in your life through transition, death or disease can be troubling. Give yourself time and space to go through the natural process of losing aspects of life. Be gentle and compassionate with yourself, for grieving is a process. There is no expiration date on a healed heart.

Only time will give you what you need. If you have lost a loved one, know they are never gone. They will live in your heart forever and their spirit is always with you. Believe you will connect with their soul again and all is truly well.

• • •

I am at peace with all of life. I allow myself to heal in the natural process of losing a loved one. I grieve the lost love but they are in my heart forever. I smile when I think of them for they are always with me in spirit and with love I send them light.

• • •

How can I be more compassionate with myself through the grieving process?

I GO FOR IT.

Do not stop yourself because of fear or limiting beliefs. Just because it hasn't been done doesn't mean its not for you to do. Go for it and give it all you've got. If the goal is in your heart and the inspiration strikes, it is time for you to take action.

There may be an area of your life where you are holding yourself back, this is a reminder to let go of all external distractions and just dive in. Go for it and persevere.

• • •

I stop making excuses and I jump in fully to the experiment of my life. I go for it and give it all I have. I tell the universe my desire and focus fully on receiving the outcome. I live my full purpose by acting out my goals. I go for it by taking action and trying new things. I do not allow any distractions. I am focused, determine and I will succeed.

• • •

What does my heart want me to go for?

I DON'T OVERTHINK MY CHOICES.

You are working too hard on trying to solve a simple problem. An outcome is possible that requires less mental power. You may be overthinking the situation and afraid to move forward. This causes a breakdown in your personal power as you retreat away from your desire. Taking action is essential for you at this point.

You have nothing to think about. You already know the answer. Go to your heart and feel your way forward. Your heart has information your head can't digest. Listen to your heart instead of overthinking situations in your life.

• • •

I give myself a mental makeover by dropping from my head to my heart. I am connected to my source energy, which is love and light. I choose to feel my answer and proceed with clarity. There is nothing to analyze or do but to feel my answer. My heart will lead me to clarity and I trust its wisdom.

• • •

What choice have I been overthinking?

I BEHAVE MY WAY TO SUCCESS.

You may have goals and desired outcomes, but your current habits might not be aligned with the results you truly desire. If you want to be fit, but you currently overeat and don't exercise, you are at a contrast from your true outcome.

Instead of focusing on self-doubt or criticizing yourself for not being able to reach your goals, look closely at your current habits. Examine your behaviors and clear up your routine. Become the person you need to be to reach success. Start to behave your way to your desired outcome.

• • •

My habits are aligned with my desired outcome. I am vibrating my dreams by being what I want to achieve. I focus my energy into my behavior, acting my way to success.

• • •

What behavior do I have that contradicts my desired outcome?

ONE DAY AT A TIME.

Let go of yesterday. Your previous actions and results have no bearing on today. Each day when you wake, you have a new opportunity to start over. If you are trying to break a habit or an addiction, compassion and love will lead the way. There is no need to overthink your previous behaviors. Instead, empower yourself by focusing on healthy actions you can take today. One day at a time will help bring you to health.

• • •

I let go of my old habits and negative thought patterns. I am connected to my desire and I make healthy choices aligned with my goal. I forgive myself for pain I caused my body. My spirit knows great learning is in my addictions and self-sabotaging habits. Instead of self-hate, I turn to love and compassion. My heart will guide my way to happiness and health.

• • •

What self-sabotaging habit can I forgive myself for?

I NOURISH MY NUDGES.

Inspiration comes to you all the time. When you get a new idea or a desire strikes your heart, it is time to nourish that nudge. Your dreams can only manifest when you take action. Pay attention to the outcome you want to receive and focus on action steps to help you get there.

• • •

I pay attention to my hearts desires. When inspiration strikes my heart, I take action immediately. There is no need to hesitate. The path will be revealed as I take action and step forward.

• • •

What nudge have I been receiving that I can nourish?

EVERYTHING ISN'T HAPPENING TO ME. IT'S HAPPENING FOR ME.

Consider that things don't happen to you, but for you. What if everything in your life right now will help you get to where your soul wants to be? Instead of resisting what is, accept it. The universe cannot mess up your big picture plans. Trust the process.

Everything in your life is part of a carefully constructed plan, created just for you, by you. Imagine your life is not a series of events outside of yourself, but a created action plan devised by yourself and the universe.

When you see the situations in your life as part of a universal plan, you will feel less burdened. If something didn't go as planned, instead of looking at the situation as a curse or setback, see it as a blessing in disguise.

• • •

I am always right where I need to be. My life is unfolding perfectly to the plan I created with the universe. If there is anything I dislike, I remove it with love. The situations in my life don't happen to me, they happen for me.

• • •

What situation is happening for me instead of to me?

I AVOID EMOTIONAL REASONING.

Don't believe what you feel is actually true. Your feelings are a guidance system, but be careful not to assume they are fact. You may be thinking your feelings are the truth, but this prevents you from seeing the honest echo of life. For example, if you feel rejected because someone turned you down, that doesn't mean you are unlovable or unworthy of other people's time. But if you believe your emotions and let them reason for you, you could block yourself from feeling confident.

• • •

I do not assume anything or pretend to know what others are thinking and feeling. I attune with my true desires and feel my feelings without attaching emotion to them. I am logical with my evaluations of situations by removing my fears and feelings. I don't take things personally. I avoid emotional reasoning.

• • •

How has emotional reasoning clouded my point of view?

MY CHOICES ARE NOT FOREVER OR FINAL.

Every choice you make is a brilliant exploration of yourself. You have an opportunity to align with your desires and learn what doesn't work for you. When you are stuck trying to make a choice, ask yourself if you are worried about the outcome? Most of the time, people fail to move forward because they think their choice will be a final move.

Nothing is every final or finished. The job you take, the relationship you enter and the home you live in are all temporary choices. Some choices last a few days, some decades. The time is irrelevant when it comes to making the choice. Just choose what feels right for you in the moment.

• • •

I make choice from a love-filled place. I do not overthink my choices I do what feels right. I embrace the journey of my life and trust that things are unfolding as they are supposed to. Every choice I make is part of a greater understanding of myself. I make choices with love and I am confident of the direction I am going.

• • •

What choice have I been afraid to make?

I ASK WHAT LESSON I CAN LEARN.

Every situation you are in is an opportunity for you to learn. If a situation keeps repeating itself, ask why am I here? What can I learn? You will receive guidance as to the lesson available for you. Instead of resisting or trying to power your way through the problem, let love guide you. The universe will support you in moving to clarity, but you must ask for help.

• • •

I am never stuck. I am not a victim of my own life's circumstances. I choose to embrace the journey of life with a focus on growth. I am always learning. If I don't know why I am in a situation I ask what can I learn. The answer is always revealed to me.

• • •

What lesson can I learn from the troubling situation?

AM I FAILING ENOUGH?

Thomas Edison said it best, "I have not failed. I've just found 10,000 ways that won't work." But with a little more perseverance, electricity was born. Never give up on your dreams. Keep going. With each new failure, you have an opportunity to achieve success.

If you aren't failing enough, you aren't trying hard enough. You may be afraid of failing, but the greatest failures lead to the greatest rewards. In order to live a passionate purpose-filled life, take more risks and don't be afraid to fail.

• • •

I am open to taking risks. I am not afraid of failing, for all failures lead me to the truth. There is no such thing as failure because I grow each time. I learn more about myself through the process of trying new things. I embrace the opportunity to grow as a person by exploring life's contrasts. I give myself permission to fail.

• • •

How can I fail harder?

I GAUGE MY HAPPINESS BY HOW MUCH FUN I AM HAVING.

Happy people gauge their happiness by the amount of fun they're having. Happy people absolutely love their jobs. For many, it doesn't feel like they work a day of their life — in fact. It's mostly play. How can you add more play into your day? When you make having fun a priority, everything feels more enjoyable. If you want to be happy beyond your wildest dreams, ask yourself if you're having fun.

• • •

I choose to play my way to happiness. When I add more fun into my life, I am happy and fulfilled. I choose work, relationships, foods and places that bring me joy. I am always having fun, for it is my number one priority.

• • •

How can I add more fun into my life?

I EXPECT GREAT RESULTS.

Expect great things for yourself. You've done a great deal of work and now it is time to step back and let the situation just be. Refocus your energy by expecting the best outcome possible. Your actions can manifest into your desires in endless ways. Let go of the how it happens, just know it will.

You are in control of your outcome. Keep focusing on the results you want. Expect great things for yourself. And don't give up. Today is a time to look inward and be honest. Where have you been settling? Now is the time to raise your standards.

• • •

I feel good about my actions and all that I do. I flow through life with effortless ease. I have high expectations and do not settle. My life is part of an ever-expansive journey. I relax into the rhyme of the process by being in the journey. I expect great things for myself and those around me. I know my intentions and actions will manifest and I will get what I want.

• • •

Where can I raise my expectations?

I AM SUCCEEDING AT LIFE.

No matter how hard your life feels right now, consider how far you've already come. When you were young, you may have felt invincible, as though you could conquer the world. Your idealistic approach to life gave you the badge of courage needed to ignore difficulties. But one life stress after another can pile on and tear down that courageous wall, leaving resentment, regret and fear.

Return to your childlike heroic self and recognize how great you are doing. When you can visit your younger self, he or she will tell you there's no need to worry because everything always works out in the end. For today, hang up your concerns and celebrate how well you are doing at life.

• • •

My life is an adventure full of exploration and awe. The situations that cause me the most anxiety today will soon fade away. I am not connected to the outcome, for I focus on what I want and expect it to come to me. I know I am doing a great job at life.

• • •

What child like sense of wonder can I bring into my adult life?

I AM NOT MY PROBLEMS.

Do you identify with your problems like the skin on your body? Your problems are not part of you. Allow them to come and go and don't identify with them. Instead of focusing on your problems, be led by the desires in your heart. The more you focus on what you want, the less of what you don't want will show up.

• • •

I take all my attention off of my dislikes and focus solely on my likes. I see the good in all situations and the possibilities are endless. My problems are not problems at all, but areas of my life that need more love. I focus on my insecurities and troubling situations with love and send light to each situation.

• • •

What problem do I spend most of my attention on? I send it love.

I DON'T HAVE TO BE HAPPY ALL THE TIME.

On any given day, the average person will have more than 50,000 thoughts. Of these, more than eighty percent can be negative. Most of these thoughts are self-deprecating. Pay attention to your thoughts and see if you are mad at yourself for not being happier. You may feel guilty because you aren't where you think you should be. Turn your negative thoughts into more loving thoughts by consciously focusing on your energy. When you are aware of your thoughts, you can control them.

• • •

I am perfectly content with where I am in this moment. I am present in my life and I feel my feelings. Every moment is a new opportunity to feel my emotions and let them work through me. I am connected to my life by being present and open to new opportunities. I remove all self-sabotaging thoughts and negativity by focusing on love.

• • •

How can I stop getting mad at myself for not being happier?

I BELONG.

No two people are created the same. This creates huge differences that make us feel alone and left out. If you struggle to feel as though you belong, know you are not alone. Every other person on the planet feels the same way, which makes us united in our differences. Embrace your unique self. The world needs you as you are.

• • •

I embrace my authentic self. I know I am different and that makes me beautiful. I don't try to fit in because I am supposed to stand out. I celebrate my unique self. I belong.

• • •

What difference about me is a unique gift?

WHEN I AM CONFIDENT NEGATIVITY CAN'T GET ME DOWN.

Haters seem to spring up when you try to do a great job. A critic of your parenting skills, your relationship status (or lack thereof), how you dress, where you live or your weight. At the end of all the haters' catcalls is an invitation to low self-esteem and self-loathing. Don't listen to the negativity.

Are negative people affecting your actions? Has someone recently attacked you for something you did? Or does the idea of someone lashing out prevent you from acting?

Ask yourself if you're actually allowing what people *could* say to stop you from following your own heart. Recognize that haters can't get to you when you feel confident and self-assured. The best way to avoid feeling victimized by the sting of negativity is to improve your relationship with yourself.

• • •

I am not what other people say I am. I am confident and secure with my own self. I don't waste time on haters or their focus on my habits. I align with my highest good and surround myself with love and light. I am confident in my skin and proud of who I am.

• • •

When do I feel the most confident?

MY BODY KNOWS HOW TO HEAL ITSELF. MY ONLY JOB IS TO GET OUT OF ITS WAY.

Your body is working hard to maintain its health. You may be criticizing yourself by attacking your body with negative thoughts, or over-stuffing it with extra food. Treat your body as a friend by showing it love and compassion. Your body is not the enemy. In fact, your body has a healing message for you. It knows how to heal itself. You just have to listen to its wisdom.

• • •

My body is my greatest tool for health. I return to wellness by sending love to my body. I trust the divine timing of my healing and I let my body be the teacher. I listen to the natural needs of my own body and give it what it needs.

• • •

My body is my greatest teacher. What message does it have for me?

I LIVE FOR THE MOMENT.

You might be working too hard to reach a particular outcome. It is good to have things to look forward to, but this moment is where life is happening. Live for this moment by being present. The greatest gift you can give yourself is to focus on the now. Stop worrying about the pain from yesterday or your what-ifs about tomorrow. Instead, be here, now.

• • •

I am still, here, now. I am present. All I have ever done has led me to right now. I am comfortable with who I am in this moment. I forgive myself, for past burdens, it was all part of my journey. For today, things are as they should be. I embrace this moment for all eternity.

• • •

What life am I missing today by reaching for tomorrow?

I MAKE HAPPINESS MY FAVORITE HABIT.

Happiness is linked to your inner desire to feel connected and loved. When you're happy, you feel confident, purposeful and in harmony with your true self. People who are genuinely happy are healthier, kinder and have better relationships. Truly happy people don't try to get happy. They just are happy because they recognize the magic of happiness is in the moment. You can train your brain to see the good in every situation and make happiness a habit.

• • •

I make happiness my favorite habit. I know I can choose to be in love or fear. Happiness is a love vibration that pulse through my body. I make healthy choices that make me feel good. I don't attack myself with criticism or negative energy. I love my life and myself. Happiness is my guiding source of inspiration.

• • •

What habit needs a happiness boost?

THE SECRET TO HAVING IT ALL IS BEING THANKFUL FOR IT ALL.

Gratitude is the life force of everything. You might be focusing too much on what you don't have. If you are comparing yourself to others and observing what they have in relation to you, realize this is a mirror to your own potential. If someone is thinner, smarter and prettier or has what you want, see this as a reflection of what is possible for you. Jealousy is a lack of love in an area of your life you desire most. If you want to have it all, be thankful for what you already have.

• • •

I am thankful for everything in my life. Even my insecurities are an opportunity for more self-awareness and compassion. I see all challengers as divine opportunities for growth. I look at my life as a creative adventure and see the results of my positive thinking. I focus on what I want and am thankful for all I have.

• • •

What insecurity can I be thankful for?

I FOCUS ON RESULTS NOT REASONS.

There is always a reason why it can't happen, or won't. And there are just as many ways in which your desire can manifest. Where you focus your attention will create your outcome. If you stop and focus on why it won't work, it will never work. Choose a positive attitude and focus on the results you want to receive. Do not waver in your attention to the outcome. When you focus on what you want, you will always get what you want.

• • •

I am dedicated to my goals. I focus on the result I want to achieve, not the reasons why they can't happen. There are infinite possibilities and ways in which my dreams will manifest. I show up daily by taking action. When I align my action with my results, I receive my desires every time.

• • •

What reasons can I abandon and replace them with results?

I AM IN TOUCH WITH MY WHY.

Why you do what you do is the most important identifier for your success. Whether you want to lose weight, quit an addiction, change jobs or relationships, find a new group of friends or start your own business, your why matters. Whatever you desire, get clear about your why.

Why you do it will help you focus clearly on your reasons to create the results you desire. When you do things from love, you are aligned with your highest truth and success will be achieved.

• • •

I am in touch with why I do what I do. I let my personal focus guide me forward. I am connected to my heart center, which is surrounded by love. I speak clearly and align my action to my intentions. Everything I do is part of my bigger plan, which connects me to my why.

• • •

What is my why for doing what I want to do?

EVERYTHING HAS A HONEYMOON STAGE.

It is fun jumping into new relationships, jobs, projects or places, but be honest with yourself and see that everything always has a honeymoon stage. If you are unhappy with an area of your life and you are planning on making a change, recognize the change will be beneficial. But until you address the core problem, the excitement of the new change will wear off.

If you are unhappy in your career and change jobs, you may be happier temporarily. As the excitement of the new wears off, you will be left with the same internal struggle. It's time to be honest with yourself: until you look at the real problem, the honeymoon phase will just mask the pain.

• • •

I am not covering up my pain by fleeing to new opportunities. I address my issues so I can heal and remove them for good. I am not in the honeymoon stage of my life. I embrace the newness but keep the excitement alive by being present and attentive with my needs.

• • •

What problem am I trying to escape by
jumping into something new?

THE DOMINO EFFECT OF
BEING KIND WILL SHOW UP
IN EVERY AREA OF MY LIFE.

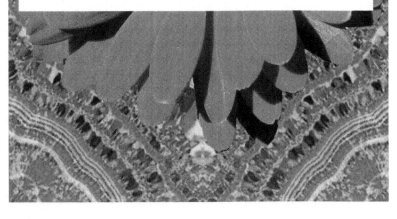

THE DOMINO EFFECT OF BEING KIND WILL SHOW UP IN EVERY AREA OF MY LIFE.

Everything you do and everyone you have met is part of your life story. Everything is always connected. When you are compassionate to others and use kindness as your approach, you will see the results of this in every area of your life.

The biggest struggles you currently face could use a little more compassion and kindness. When you approach problems with an attitude of kindness and love, you will get results faster. Think of your current struggles and send kindness to them.

• • •

I am kind. I am love. I focus my attention on being there for others through compassion and love. I know that being kind to others ripples out into every area of my life. When I am nice to others, I feel good about myself. I know we help each other feel more grounded and safe because kindness wins.

• • •

How can I be more kind to others?

WHAT I DO TODAY HAS THE POTENTIAL TO IMPROVE ALL OF MY TOMORROWS.

Your actions right now are the most important. Don't worry about yesterday or anything that has happened in your past. From a manifesting standpoint, the only thing that matters is your attention in this moment. Focus on the outcome and achieving what you desire. Pay attention to your thoughts and how they align with your desired outcome. What you do today is important. It will determine your tomorrow.

• • •

Starting now, I focus forward. I align my energy with love and support. I will achieve my goal by taking action today. I let go of my past, for today is the only day that matters. It is never too late to start again. Today is my new beginning. What I do today has the potential to improve all my tomorrows.

• • •

What can I do today to improve my tomorrow?

I AM AT PEACE WITH WHERE I AM.

It's going to be okay. The majority of your thoughts have been focused on the problem. You have not given yourself a mental break. Forgive yourself and use self-compassion as a tool to move you out of this difficult situation. Healing can occur when you take your focus off the situation. When you accept where you are, you can begin to move forward into where you want to be.

• • •

I am at peace. There is nothing to change or shift. Through every experience, I learn more about my true self. I am not wounded or damaged. All is in right order. Everything I experience is part of my deepest heart's desire. I am growing and learning more about myself and that is the greatest gift of all. I am at peace with where I am, for it is helping me become who I want to be.

• • •

What do I need to make peace with?

I'M OVER THIS LESSON.
I AM DONE.

Life is like a giant classroom. You get to take courses and study different topics: self-worth, humility, financial security, boredom, love, forgiveness and so on. If you are currently in a situation that feels troublesome, ask what you can learn. You will get your lesson and move through. If you get to a place where you are over it, declare you are done. "I don't want to learn this anymore," And move on. Ask yourself what you want to learn and focus on a new topic. Maybe you are sick of trying so hard to please others. Maybe your efforts have exhausted you. Declare you are over this lesson and move on. Start to put your needs first and you will feel the approval you wanted all along.

• • •

I am over this. I am sick of feeling this way and choose not to vibrate at this level anymore. I leave this lesson behind and embrace new opportunities to grow. I am no longer stuck in my fear and I remove what no longer works in my life. I am over this lesson. I am done.

• • •

What lesson am I done with?

NONE OF MY EXPERIENCES DEFINE WHO I AM.

You are the sum of all your experiences, but that's not who you are. You are more than what you go through. Don't let your burdens bring you down. The problems you face do not define you. Your focus is not on the situation, but how you perceive the situation.

See each experience as an exploration of self and an opportunity for you to practice more love. Your choices align with your greater plan, but don't get stuck into thinking you are what you do.

• • •

I am more than my experiences. I am not what I do. I am bigger than my expressions of life. I believe in my greatness and challenge myself to try new things. When I try new experiences, I grow and become more of who I really want to be.

• • •

What experience have I been wrapping my identity in?

I COMPLIMENT MYSELF DAILY.

Your inner dialogue is exhausted from all of the self-sabotage and hate. The negative energy you hold about yourself is hurting your heart. You are far more beautiful, kind, intelligent and loving than you realize. Release all the negativity you have with love and compassionate focus. When you can turn your negative energy into loving light, you will feel more connected to your best self.

Compliment yourself instead of turning to negativity. Go a full day without talking bad about yourself. Each time you fall into negative self-talk, be aware and give yourself a compliment. When you are aware of your thoughts, they create your reality. Turn your negative energy into positive light.

• • •

I am aware of my conscious thoughts and I align with love. I choose positive thoughts and I talk nicely about myself to myself. I compliment myself by celebrating my uniqueness. I let go of my insecurities and replace them with love.

• • •

What area of my life needs the most compliments?

I ALLOW MY IMAGINATION TO EXPLORE OPTIONS FOR DIFFICULT SITUATIONS.

If you are in a difficult situation, consider a more playful approach. You are overthinking the problem, which is preventing you from seeing a result. Instead of focusing on the situation, turn to your imagination and let it lead the way. Your imagination is more powerful than any logic. Trust your imagination and let it lead the way.

• • •

My imagination helps me solve problems in my life. Instead of overthinking it or overanalyzing outcomes, I turn to my playful heart and imagine different situations playing out. When I am in touch with my true self, my imagination is active and full of love.

• • •

What problem can I solve by tapping into my imagination?

I BELIEVE THINGS ARE SHIFTING IN MY FAVOR.

It doesn't matter where you come from, what your background is or what has happened in the past. You have the capacity to turn things around. Believe things are falling into place and everything is working out in your favor.

Focus on the steps you've taken to help put yourself in a better position. You've made some great choices and your ship is coming in. Plan out your next steps and focus on the long-term solution. Review your focus with enthusiasm and you will achieve what you truly desire. Trust that all of the work you've done will produce wonderful results. There is nothing to do, no need to worry. Sometimes it takes a while to see a return on your investments, both energetic and financial. Be patient and know it is on its way to you.

• • •

My ship has come in. All of my hard work is now rewarded. This is a time of great celebration, as my efforts have been achieved. I believe in the power of my future and everything is now turning out for the best. I believe things are always shifting in my favor and the world is on my side.

• • •

What evidence that things are working out can I celebrate?

INDECISION DOES NOT LIVE IN MY HEART.

You may be experiencing a pause in action. Now is not the time to rest. Be bold and assert yourself and your true desires. Don't let indecision derail you or prevent you from moving forward. When you are indecisive, it is because you are overthinking the outcome or worried about what others will think. Instead, drop to your heart to gain the clarity you seek.

• • •

I am ambitious with my focus and I move forward with clarity. I don't overthink situations because I release my fear and act from a place of love. All of my choices are guided by love. I am supported and my heart will show me the way.

• • •

What desire needs more clarity?

I CAN CHANGE DIRECTIONS.

You may be called to look at your life and refocus your direction. Every day is an opportunity to start again. All of your past experiences have lead you to where you are today. Remove all regret and frustration associated with feeling as though you aren't where you should be.

Now is an ideal time to look at your own past and make changes that will put you on a fresh path. Don't judge your past with criticism, but seek to understand what choices helped you gain clarity to move forward today.

• • •

I accept my life as an exploration of self and personal discovery. I am always growing and changing, which leads me to deeper understandings of my truth. Every choice I have ever made is part of a big picture plan. I align with my heart to help me move forward. It is time to change directions and let go of my past. I am open to living my life in new exciting ways. I take on new directions in my life with joy and confidence.

• • •

What new beginning am I being called to?

I AM ALWAYS GROWING AND NEEDING NEW TEACHERS.

Pay attention to the guidance you receive right now. You are living your answered prayer. You may have yearned for new teachers, books, courses, friends or situations to come into your life. You may notice your past approach and relationships no longer work the way they use to.

You may be on a spiritual path of new self-discovery, looking for deeper understanding of yourself and the world. Your old way of doing things or relating to others no longer feels the same. This is because you are always growing. Instead of holding onto old behaviors and people, allow yourself to spread your wings and fly. You are coming into a new time of great understanding. Allow yourself to be guided and open to new teachers.

• • •

I am always changing and growing into who I am supposed to be. I recognize my need for greater awareness and I seek out mentors, teachers, authors, friends and situations that align with my highest intention. I release old patterns, people and ways of being so I can welcome in the new energy that supports my growth and expansion. I release my old habits and embrace a more loving perspective.

• • •

What teacher am I being called to study from?

THINGS GO GRAY WHEN
I FORGET TO PLAY.

You are taking yourself too seriously. The situation you are in may requires a less constricted approach, meaning don't look at it as black and white. When you struggle to find meaning in a troubling situation, you are often looking at it from one point of view. Instead of overthinking what happened or what will happen, play and you will watch the situation resolve itself.

When you take your attention off of what bothers you, the experience has time to heal. The world is full of opportunities for you to lighten up and be more light-hearted. Things will naturally fall into place when you play with the world.

• • •

I play my way to happiness. I am connected to my joyful self and I bring more fun into everything I do. The situations that cause me the most stress are healed by my loving attention to the light-hearted nature of life. I don't take myself so seriously and this lets the situation heal.

• • •

How can I bring more fun into a troubling situation?

I PROTECT MY ENERGY.

There is an energetic shift happening on the planet all the time. As things shift, you feel the vibration. Many people feel this vibration and turn to fear and negativity. You can choose to disengage with this low energy and attach yourself to love and light. Possibilities are open to you when you follow the light.

When you protect your energy, you become a source of inspiration for others. You are a light worker on the edge of thought, helping others become their best selves. This is a natural evolution of your own self-development. You grow more into who you really are and allow your true light to shine. Be clear with your focus and align with love and inspiration.

• • •

I am protected by love and light. I turn away all negativity and only allow love into my life. I am inspired and connected to my joy. When I align my intentions with my soul's purpose, I am a light worker for others. I hold the positive intentions and send peace and love out into the world. I am love and inspiration and I am connected to my truth. I protect my energy by aligning with love.

• • •

How can I protect my energy form negative thoughts and people?

I DESERVE BETTER.

You are sacrificing you true self in an area of your life. Look closely and stop overshadowing the truth with habits and your own fears. You deserve better. Look carefully at all of your relationships and see who you are pretending to be in order to make others happy. This can be in a relationship with your self as well. Stop the negative self-talk and transform it with compassion. It is time you respect yourself and believe in your worth.

• • •

I deserve the highest form of love from my self and others. I only choose positive, loving people to share my life with. I am focused on health and happiness and my behaviors align with this truth. I remove what doesn't serve me. I am aligned with my true worth. I deserve greatness and I allow it to flow to me.

• • •

Where do I deserve better?

I DO MY PART.

Pablo Picasso said, "Inspiration exists, but it has to find you working." Making your dreams come true is not a passive process. You have to do the work and show up for your part. Sitting on your meditation pillow, repeating mantras or visualizing (although good methods), will never produce the outcome – until you take action and do the work.

You must step forward and be in the process of creating in order for the universe to support you. Do your part and show up fully. If you feel stuck and don't know which action to take, declare this out load. Throw your hand up and say, "I need guidance. What action should I take?" The first inspiration that comes to you is the action for you to move on. Do your part and the universe will show up and reward your efforts.

• • •

I am showing up for my dreams by taking action daily. I am aligned with the universe and we create together. I do my part and the universe supports all my actions. I am dedicated to my plan and I focus forward.

• • •

How can I show up fully and take action?

WE ARE ALL CONNECTED BY OUR THOUGHTS.

You've been thinking about a person lately and wondering about them. This person who keeps coming into your mind is connected to you through your thoughts. That person is sending you love at this moment. Send them love in return.

Maybe you've been worried about a relationship or judging yourself for the way things worked out. This is a time for you to surround the relationship with light and let love heal the open wounds. Trust that the relationship was exactly what it was supposed to be for all involved. Forgive him or her and yourself, and be open to the presence of the love.

• • •

I am connected to others by my thoughts. When I think about them, they are thinking about me too. I send them love and light. I did nothing wrong. The relationship is as it was supposed to be.

• • •

Who can I send love to?

GROWTH SPURTS INDUCE FEAR, BUT THERE IS NOTHING TO BE AFRAID OF.

You may be on a spiritual or self-development path and awakening to a new level of your potential. When this happens, you step into a new area of life, one you have never experienced. This will bring fear to the surface.

Insecurities that have not been addressed will show up and scream louder than before. Be kind to yourself and know this is part of the process. Your growth spurt is a beautiful thing. Do not shy away from your greatness by letting your fear stop you. When you address your fear, you can move through it.

• • •

I am not limited by my fears. My thoughts are loving and aligned with my truth and I am in integrity. When I grow and become more of who I really am, my insecurity will reveal fears. This is part of my heroic journey and there is nothing to be afraid of. The fears are just surface lies trying to keep me playing small. I embrace my truth and ignore the fear, for my dreams are worth it and I am full of unlimited potential.

• • •

What fear do I have to address in order to reach my goal?

THEY ARE NOT JUDGING ME.

You spend a generous amount of time worrying about what others think of you. When you are in public, you assume others are thinking about you and judging you. This thought process keeps you from being true to yourself.

You are so worried about what they think of you that you are taking attention off of yourself and your ability to reach your own potential. When you see others who give you a discerning eye or a disapproving glance, recognize they are reflecting your own insecurities.

If you feel unlovable, you may hear rude comments. It isn't the comments that made you feel unlovable. This was already your experience of self. To feel more confident in social situations, focus on self-love and approval.

• • •

Other people do not control me. When others say something that hurts my feelings, I know it is not about me. I can't control what others say to me, but I can control my reaction to what they say. I choose self-love and I approve of myself. There is only one of me in all eternity. I am uniquely me. I am nonjudgmental and judgment-free.

• • •

What steps will I take to release judgment?

I CAN'T CHANGE WHAT
I DON'T ADDRESS.

Get honest with yourself about everyone and every situation in your life. What is not working? It is time to stop making excuses and address situations and relationships? Be accountable for your life and relationships. Do not compromise.

Self-destructive behaviors will become worse if you don't acknowledge them. Be honest with where you are right now so you can address what needs fixing.

• • •

I am accountable for all of my experiences. I am honest with myself about what is not working and I release it with love. I take full responsibility for my direction in life by reassessing where I am. If there is anything that doesn't work for me, I let it go. I trust the situation will be replaced with love and positive energy.

• • •

What do I need to address that I have been avoiding?

THERE IS NO REALITY, ONLY PERCEPTION.

You have a view of life that is personal to you and filtered through your beliefs, actions and experiences. Acknowledge your past, but don't be controlled by it. To live a happy life, recognize your filters and be compassionate so that they don't distort your perceptions or mislead your decision-making. You might be viewing the world through a filter of past events, which controls your present and dictates your future. Take care not to let fears from the past replay.

If you don't acknowledging you have fears or limiting beliefs from the past that could be controlling your behavior, you will feel powerless. Let your perceptions be fresh and new and grounded in fact, not in history.

• • •

I am not a victim of my past. I understand my past is in my past. I focus on my present and make choices from a loving place. I am aligned with my heart's desires and I let love lead the way. I do not judge myself for my beliefs or past experiences. Instead, I look closely at my filters of the world and remove limiting beliefs and thought limitations.

• • •

What filter has distorted my reality?

I TEACH PEOPLE HOW TO TREAT ME.

Look at all of your relationships and see what they have in common: You. How do people in those relationships treat you? You either show people to treat you with love and respect or you don't. You are, on some level, responsible for any mistreatment in your life. You have, on some level, allowed it to persist.

Instead of blaming or complaining about your relationships, own your true self-worth and stand up for yourself with dignity and pride. You can refocus any relationship. Even patterns that have persisted for fifteen years can be address by you negotiating your real worth. Commit to yourself from a place of love and light, not fear and doubt. Let your relationships be full of love.

• • •

I commit to raising the vibration of all of my relationships. I teach people how to treat me because I show them my worth. I don't stand for harm. I only have supportive caring relationships. I am connected to light and full of love. I love myself and this extends out into all my relationships.

• • •

How have I taught other people to treat me?

SITUATIONS DON'T HURT.
EXPECTATIONS DO.

Take a moment to reflect on what you wanted to happen. If there are situations causing you pain, look at what your expectations were. Did you want something to happen that didn't? Or maybe things didn't work out according to your plan. Expectations hurt your ability to enjoy life and accept the process.

When you set a goal, release the expectation and focus on the feeling instead of the outcome. How does it feel to feel your goal in action? This is the energy you want to hold. Leave the how and when to the universe. You will always get exactly what you need when you need it.

• • •

I release all expectations and allow myself to be in the flow of life. I embrace the journey and let things unfold naturally. I am in no hurry and there is no rush to get where I want to go. The situations I am in are part of my life plan. I accept them as though I had chosen them myself. I release all expectations and trust things are as they should be.

• • •

What expectations did I have of the situation
causing me the most pain?

THERE IS PLENTY OF TIME.

You may feel frustrated because what you want has not yet arrived. When you are manifesting and working toward your dreams, instant gratification is what you seek. But patience is about being at peace with the process. Recognize there is a divine timing to your desire and it will come to you at the perfect time.

When you are impatient, it energetically holds the process. Because you focus on what you want not being here, you actually put more attention to the lack. Breathe in deeply and ask yourself what you still need to learn. You will receive guidance to help you around the situation.

• • •

There is plenty of time and I am in no hurry. My dreams will manifest at the perfect time and in right order. I release all expectations around my life and goals and know I am being divinely led. There is always plenty of time.

• • •

What am I rushing?

MY HAPPILY EVER AFTER IS ME.

Romantic relationships are a beautiful part of life. But even marriages will end. The only person you are with forever is yourself. Stop chasing love and looking for happily ever after. Love yourself unconditionally and you will find the love you desire. You can become your own best friend and fall in love with you as a partner. When you love your own company, you will no longer be searching outside of yourself. You will feel peaceful and connected.

• • •

I flood my body with love, for I am love and light. I connect to the universe's infinite pool of love and all there is. I am the one I have been looking for. I don't have to seek out love in romantic relationships, for I am enough as I am. The love I give myself bubbles out into all of my interactions. I am full of peace and purpose as I shine my light out into the world. I honor my desires and reach happiness through self-acceptance and love.

• • •

How can I celebrate my declaration of self-love?

ISSUES ARE JUST OLD PATTERNS I NEED TO ADDRESS.

When an issue arises in your life, it is an opportunity to look at your current habits. Look to see what is working and release what no longer resonates. Be loving to your habits and address what is causing you more harm. If there is a habit that no longer supports you, it is time to release it. Recognize you are the creator of your own life experience, so you can change your experience at any time.

All of your habits have served you for one reason: to help you learn more about yourself. And they will fulfill a purpose. Release the old patterns with love and be open to finding more supportive ways to fulfill those needs.

• • •

I take time to look at my habits and release what is no longer serving me. I know all of my habits have served a purpose at one time, but with honesty and loving light, I can release the burden. I know the universe will help me release fear associated with leaving patterns behind. I welcome in the new opportunity for expansive growth.

• • •

What habit am I ready to get rid of?

I ALIGN MY THOUGHTS WITH LOVE.

Moment-to-moment thinking is where your power lies. When you talk down to yourself, you hurt your capacity to let love in. But each moment, you can cultivate an awareness of expansion by catching your negative voice in action. When you hear your inner dialog turn to negativity, surround it with love and repeat kind words. "You are doing the best you can and it is all going to be okay." You will get clear results with consistency.

The more you can stop negativity and fear-based thoughts, the happier you will be. It doesn't matter what yesterday held or what your thoughts were growing up. The only place you ever have any power is right here, right now. Align your thoughts with love.

• • •

The place I can make the most change in my life is right here, right now, with my thoughts. I align my energy to love and release all negative fear-based thoughts. I speak kindly to myself and uplift others with love.

• • •

What is a loving thought about myself?

EVERYTHING IS RELATIVE.

Every day, you are changing and growing. The person you were when you stepped into the current situation causing your frustration is not the same person you are today. The situation has helped you learn more about what is important to you. It is necessary to reevaluate and see if your current situation is serving you.

Everything is relative and part of your life plan. When you can look objectively at situations, you will see the path to take. Be willing to let go of situations that once caused you pleasure but now cause pain.

• • •

I understand everything is relative and part of a bigger life plan. The universe supports me. My decision to move forward is based from love. I learn from all of my situations and see the power in letting go.

• • •

What situations have I outgrown?

I FOUND MY HAPPY.

You may be trying to get happy, but the happiness you desire is already within you. Instead of making your happiness contingent on external forces or a future event yet to manifest, choose to be happy in this moment. Focus all of your energy into gratitude and fill your heart with love.

All of the work you do, the books you read, the course and self-development tools are part of your divine life plan. Release the need to get there and have the instant hit of "having it all figured out." Self-improvement comes from a compassionate approach and one that can be a joyful journey. Enjoy the teachers you resonate with and let your happy shine through. You already have what you seek. Just let it be and trust you have arrived.

• • •

I open my heart to happiness and joy. I embrace all of the good in my life and I am thankful for what is. I feel loved and I am supported. All of my dreams are coming true and I choose happiness right now.

• • •

What is working great in my life?

INSTEAD OF TRYING TO GET ATTENTION, I GIVE IT.

You may be trying to get the attention of another person but feel like he or she is not seeing you for who you are. Your attitude may be desperate or needy. Instead of trying to get attention, try to give it.

By giving what you seek, you will, in return, get what you want. Giving attention to others is part of your soul's purpose. To be of service and help others allows you to get out of your own way and serve.

• • •

Beautiful things do not need attention. They are as they are. I am a beautiful person who does good deeds. I do not need attention for my acts of kindness. I seek out ways in which I can be of service and help others. Instead of trying to get attention, I give it to others.

• • •

How can I be of service?

I'M NOT AFRAID TO INVEST IN MY DREAMS.

Putting in energy, time and financial resource into something you believe in will never lead you astray. When your heart and head are aligned and you're focused on your desire, you give it all you got. Investing in your dreams is investing in yourself. When you show up for your dreams, you are saying you matter.

A farmer does not yell at his crop to grow faster. He knows there is a season of growing and a season of harvest. If you are investing in your dream, give yourself time to see the harvest. Don't abandon your dream because it isn't growing fast enough. Great things take time to develop, but when you water them with love, you will be rewarded in more ways than you can ever imagine. Don't give up on yourself or your dreams.

• • •

I spend time, money and energy on the things that are important to me. I am not afraid to invest in my dreams because I know I will see the return. I believe in my heart I am doing the right thing for me, so I move forward with confidence, faith and a knowing that all of my actions will be rewarded. The universe supports my dream by watering it with love. I will see the rewards soon and all of my hard work will be worth it.

• • •

What dream will I invest in?

I AM SELECTIVE WITH MY CHOICES.

Becoming more selective with your activities, friends, social engagements and habits will serve you right now. When you are selective with how you spend your time, you place specialness on what you value. If you are over-extending yourself or giving away to much of your time, your energy will be depleted.

Having a close group of sincere friends versus a wide range of people you kind of know will help you feel more connected and grounded. Make more choices with a selective process. Choosing how you spend your time and with whom cultivates self-respect.

• • •

I love myself enough to do what I want when I want. I don't waste time on people, places or things that waste my energy. I focus on loving thoughts and spend my time with people I love. Together we accomplish great things because we support one another with compassion, hope and joy.

• • •

What choice can I be more selective with?

PROCRASTINATION IS A DEAD DESIRE.

Procrastination happens when you are not in touch with your heart's desires. Any activity worthy of your effort should be approached with love and tackled with gusto. You don't have to do it all in one day, but taking it in bits and pieces can help.

When you procrastinate, you show yourself your activities do not matter, which sends a message to yourself that you are unworthy of your desires. If you put off projects, find a way to tap into the reason you love it. This will help you feel connected to the project and help you move forward with more clarity.

• • •

I do not waste time on frivolous things. I am focused on my plan and I do not procrastinate. When things need to be done, I do them with care. I take one step at a time to reach my goals. I focus on mini-goals within the big goal to help me conquer my fears. I am in touch with my desires, which leads me forward.

• • •

What have I been procrastinating?

I EXPRESS HUMILITY.

When you shift directions, change carriers, relationships, move or try something new, you will be stepping out of your comfort zone. Letting go of how others perceive you will serve you well through all changes. Maybe you were fired from your job and you took a position at a new company that pays a lot less. Express humility.

Perhaps you went through a tough divorce and the other person has remarried, but you are still single. Express humility. Being humble through your life changes will help you surrender to what is. You can release expectations about how your life should look or how it was supposed to turn out by returning to your heart center, which is humble and full of humility.

• • •

I express divine grace through my detachment to self. I am not my situations or my problems. I am separate from my life drama. I express kindness and love to all by accepting myself as I am today. I am humble and honest with who I am and where I stand. I express humility.

• • •

How can I be more humble?

I DON'T HANG ONTO MOMENTS.

Hanging onto moments once they have gone will keep you from moving forward. There are joyful lessons to be learned in your current experience, but hanging onto the past keeps you from receiving these rewards. Life goes on and will unfold ever expansively. But when you spend your time thinking about the past, you hurt your present and future.

Be honest with yourself and see if you are hanging onto something in your past. It could be a relationship, a job, the money you earn or a place you lived. Whatever the situation, if you are stuck in a moment, you will invite more shame into your life. When you bring your attention to the now, you invite others into your life. Let go of past moments so you can be present in this moment.

• • •

I am present in my life and free of past burdens. I don't hang onto memories or replay them in the present. I am focused on my current reality and free of fear. I am happy and focused on this moment, for right now is all I have.

• • •

What moment do I keep replaying in my mind?

I LISTEN TO MY FEELINGS.

Your feelings are telling you the truth. It may be difficult to face the current reality, but know your feelings are being honest with you. Your feelings are an emotional guidance system that can help you know right from wrong.

Your current situation is resolved when you listen to your feelings. Don't second-guess yourself or what you feel. Your gut feeling is accurate. If you feel conflicted, go to your heart and ask what you should do. You will receive loving guidance to help you move forward.

• • •

My feelings are my saviors. They guide me to safety and help me make the right choice. My feelings don't lie. They are always accurate. I trust myself and my feelings are guiding me home. I respect my inner voice as it connects me to the universe. I listen to my feelings and trust their guidance.

• • •

What are my feelings trying to tell me?

THERE ARE NO ACCIDENTS.

You are on the right path as long as you stay focused on your heart's desire. You may feel like you have gotten off track, but there are no mistakes. Everything you are currently experiencing is part of your ultimate life plan.

Realize your negative thoughts and their associated emotions result from your mind. No matter what terrible choices you've made, or what horrible event has happened, you have the choice to see it as a blessing or a curse. The universe is always leading you to path of greater understanding and reward. See the opportunities in all situations and you will be free of worry.

• • •

I see everything as an opportunity for growth and awareness. I am living my life as an example of what's possible and I live it on purpose. There are no accidents or wrong turns. Every step I take is part of a perfect plan devised by my higher self. The universe supports me and guides me to freedom.

• • •

What mistake can I forgive myself for?

THIS IS NOT MY PRACTICE LIFE.

No more excuses. It's time to get it done. This is not a practice life. Right now this is all you have. Give your life the meaning you crave. It is your mission to give it all you've got. When you blame, worry or make excuses about why it can't be done, someone else with less is doing more.

Give yourself permission to be all you really are meant to be and you will amaze yourself. A desire deep in your heart is ready to come out. Show the world what you are made of by being true to your heart's desires.

• • •

I am capable of everything I put my mind to. I achieve greatness by giving it my all. This is not my practice life. This is the real deal. I show up with gusto and align with my heart's purpose. I am love and a reflection of light. I share all that is good.

• • •

What do I need to give myself more credit for?

THE LESS I KNOW ABOUT *"HOW,"* THE BETTER.

Having a can-do attitude and a go get 'em spirit will give you the results you desire. Go for it and make it happen. When you have a new project or goal you are working on, you may hesitate because you don't know what path to take. The path that has been paved before might not work best for you. Just because it has worked for others doesn't mean you don't have a different plan.

Don't be afraid to go your own way and carve out a new plan. The world's greatest innovators, inspirational teachers and thought leaders do things their own way. Instead of looking to see what has been done or what is possible, believe in your heart that you can do it and go for it with your imagination and knowledge.

• • •

I am not afraid of my own greatness. I shine my light bright and do what works for me. I refuse to accept others' opinions and views about my life and direction. I do what is right for me and what feels good for me. No one can stand in my way when I align with my truth. My plan is unique to me. I fearlessly move forward.

• • •

What do I want to do that hasn't been done?

WHATEVER WILL BE WILL BE.

The future is not yours to see. What is unfolding is part of a divine plan that will work in your favor. There is no need for you to see the whole picture. Trust the process and be in the journey. When you worry about the future and try to control the outcome, you stop yourself from living your life fully.

Whatever will be will be. It is part of your truth. Trust you will get what you need when you need it, but not a moment sooner. Everything in your life will always work out. Be in the journey of your life and focus forward with compassion and joy.

• • •

I have goals I work toward but I don't hold on or try to manipulate the outcome. I co-create with the universe and trust I will get what I need when I need it. The future is not for me to see, but I am comfortable in the unknown. I focus forward, living from my heart. All is in right order and everything will work out in my favor. It always does.

• • •

How can I be more present in this moment?

I REFUSE TO STAND IN MY OWN WAY. I BELIEVE IN ALL I CAN BE.

You are more powerful, focused and capable than you realize. Now more than ever, you are in a position to reach your potential. Pay attention to your senses as they come to life and guide you forward. Your intuition is talking to you. Listen to its message. You are being guided into the next right step, but you must know you are capable.

Everything you have ever done has prepared for this moment. You're ready. Believe in yourself and you will see the manifestation of your heart's truest desire. Hold that faith and let it guide you forward. Only you can allow others to take away your hopes and dreams. Don't get derailed by others. Focus your intentions with love and surround yourself with light.

• • •

Everything is connected and part of my divine plan. I am more aware and connected than I have ever been and this moment is what matters. I refuse to stand in my own way. I believe in everything I can be, and I live my truth daily.

• • •

How have I been standing in my own way?

I REFUSE TO STAND IN MY OWN WAY.
I BELIEVE IN ALL THAT I CAN BE.

MY FUTURE STARTS TODAY.

Everything you have ever wanted to be is possible. You can start fresh and refocus any time. Today is the most important day of your life, for it determines the rest of your journey. What you do today is the path to your tomorrow.

When you are present in this moment, you have all the power, focus, skills and energy you need. Release your past burdens and focus fully on today. Your future is unwritten, but it can turn out better than you ever imagined with your action today.

• • •

I am aligned with love. Every action I take is guided with love to help me become more of who I see myself becoming. Tomorrow is unwritten. But I can control my outcome by the actions I take today. I take loving action and direct myself into happiness with light.

• • •

What action can I take to create my ideal future?

I PLAY WITH THE WORLD.

The world is your playground. Do not settle or sit back and wait for things to happen. You are at the forefront of your life, in the driver's seat of your destiny. Create your life by aligning with your truth. Only you know what is right for you.

Let go of all limitations from others, limiting beliefs and external forces that try to derail you. You have the capacity to live life on your own terms and it starts with you playing with the world. Explore your heart's desires and have fun in the glorious adventure of life.

• • •

My needs are met and everything is in right order. All I desire is on its way to me. There is nothing left for me to do but play with the world.

• • •

How will I celebrate my life now?

ABOUT THE AUTHOR

Shannon Kaiser has been called a modern thought-leader on the rise by *Café Truth*, and is among the Top 25 Most Influential Wellness Experts, according to *MindBodyGreen*.

She is the bestselling author of *Find Your Happy, an Inspirational Guide to Loving Life to Its Fullest*, and a six-time contributing author to *Chicken Soup for The Soul*.

Shannon is an inspirational author, speaker, travel writer, teacher and life coach who left her successful career in advertising to follow her heart and be a writer. Her unique and adventurous take on self-help inspires people to take risks and embrace the unknown so they may live openly and courageously from their heart.

Her website, PlayWithTheWorld.com, was named in the top 100 self-help blogs and the top 75 personal growth websites on the Internet by the Institute for the Psychology of Eating.

Shannon's sought-after ideas have been featured in media outlets across the world, such as *Good Morning America*, *Good Day New York*, *Inside Edition*, *HuffPost Live*, *Australian Vogue*, *Health Magazine*. She is also an online columnist for *Huffington Post*, *MindBodyGreen*, *Yahoo Voices*, *Healing Lifestyles & Spas*, *Examiner*, News.com.AU, *Tiny Buddha* and *The Daily Love*.

When she's not traveling on assignment or playing with the world, she lives in Portland, Oregon, with her adventure buddy, her dog, Tucker. She is finishing her next book, *Adventures for Your Soul* (Berkley Press, 2015).

Stay Connected:

From inspirational articles to insightful blogs, podcasts, workshops and more, playwiththeworld.com is full of tools to encourage more confidence in your daily life.

Facebook: @ShannonKaiserWrites
Twitter: @shannonlkaiser
Pinterest: @Playwtworld
Instagram: @shannonkaiserwrites

For more inspiration
Visit her website PlayWithTheWorld.com

WORK WITH SHANNON

COACHING:

Do you feel stuck or are you looking for more clarity? Private coaching with Shannon is an empowering experience. She has coached thousands of people all around the world with her unique method of intuitive guidance, combined with life experience and practical tools. Clients are guided to achieve an authentic connection to their best self and tap into true happiness and inner peace.

For private coaching, business coaching and corporate workshops:
Contact Shannon at Coach@PlayWithTheWorld.com.

AUTHOR MENTORSHIP:

This is a breakthrough mentorship-coaching program for aspiring authors. The coaching program will educate you on all aspects of the publishing industry and help you create a solid plan to reach your literary goals. The mentorship-training program shows you, step-by-step, how to succeed in the literary world, get clear about your writing goals and turn your passion to write into a money-making, life-changing lifestyle.

For mentorship options:
Contact Shannon at Coach@PlayWithTheWorld.com.

SPEAKING:

Shannon is available for speaking engagements, corporate workshops and media interviews.

For Press Inquiries: **info@playwiththeworld.com**
For Speaking – **Shannon@playwiththeworld.com**

Or *All American Speakers*-
Contact Joanna Finney – joanna@allamericanentertainment.com.

ABOUT THE EDITOR

Rebecca T. Dickson is a bestselling author and award-winning editor and writing coach. A former reporter and editor for the top small daily in New England, she turned her passion for words into a career early.

She is the bestselling author of *The Definitive Guide to Writing on Your Terms*, a #1 Amazon bestseller on how to find your writing voice and get the words out. She is also a prolific ghostwriter and writing coach for the elite contributors to *The Chiron Review* and *The Paris Review*.

Rebecca left a successful journalism career to help other writers be their best. Her unique take on the writing and editing process helps struggling authors end the struggle. She inspires people to take risks and embrace the process so they can write without fear.

When she's not crafting words and polishing prose for others, she's working on her third book for writers, tentatively called *How to Write More Words with Less Stress*.

She lives in Webster, New Hampshire, with her husband and two children.

Find out more at her website, RebeccaTDickson.com.

ABOUT THE COVER ART

A note from the author: It was important to me to design a cover that felt as expansive as the process of reading this book. My first book, *Find Your Happy*, had signature red boots jumping in the air on a dark cloudy day. That was significant because it represented the action steps we need to take to pull ourselves into a happy state. It also signaled to the joy of the process of self-development and finding happiness. This book is an evolution of healing and being able to receive love, light, inspiration and truth.

The hands on the cover are in a meditative prayer pose, which allows the process of happiness to soak in. When hands are faced upward to the sky, this is the receiving energy mosw, which allows the healing to resonate on a deeper level. The glitter, of course (aside from being fabulous and making me smile), is about celebrating the arrival of happiness, your inner child in joy and coming into your own true self. Thank you for taking this journey into peace and practicing your happy every day.

Cover Art Photo:

The photo on the cover was taken by Nick Ray
http://herlovelyheart.com/

I teamed up with this company because we share the same philosophy that self-development is an essential key to achieving your dreams.

Her Lovely Heart is a humming rhythm of inspiration and encouragement that nurtures photographers and other artists in the pursuit of running their own businesses. The company's resources and training are born out of a desire to help people build a business around their passion, while also keeping creative juices flowing. They believe building your own business can be the most creative thing you'll ever do, and you should have fun along the way.

Notes

Notes

Notes

Notes

Notes

Notes

<u>Notes</u>

<u>Notes</u>

Notes

Notes

Notes

64903154R00243

Made in the USA
Lexington, KY
23 June 2017